Everyday Life in
EARLY IMPERIAL
CHINA

1 Bronze mirror made in the official workshops (see p. 189): reverse
side, with symbols of the cosmic order and inscriptions (see pp. 116f.)

Everyday Life in
EARLY IMPERIAL
CHINA

During the Han Period 202 BC–AD 220

MICHAEL LOEWE

Drawings by Eva Wilson

DORSET PRESS
New York

This edition published by Dorset Press,
a division of Marboro Books Corporation,
by arrangement with
B.T. Batsford Ltd.
1988 Dorset Press

ISBN 0-88029-177-X

Printed in the United States of America
M 9 8 7 6 5 4 3 2 1

Preface

Ideally, a volume in this series should set out the day-to-day conditions of the lives led by the majority of the people who lived in the time and place that is specified in the title; but unfortunately the nature of the evidence at our disposal strictly limits the success with which this purpose can be achieved. When Chinese literature refers to conditions of daily life, it tends to depict the ways of that small minority of the inhabitants who lived in comparatively luxurious and abnormal circumstances. Both the authors of these writings and their readers were in all probability members of that minority; and while some of them may well have been deeply interested in the basic occupations of most of their fellow-men, they would have little reason to leave detailed descriptions of commonplace sights such as a village or a slum, a goods waggon or a grainbarge. Inscriptions do not add much to our knowledge of daily life; and perhaps the most valuable archaeological evidences that we possess are the models of figures, houses, well-heads or other objects that were buried in the tombs of the more prominent members of the community. In general we have at our disposal less evidence regarding the fundamental features of Han life than we have for the elegancies enjoyed by a few rather exceptional members of society.

Any attempt, then, to describe everyday life in Han China will be hampered by a scarcity of essential information; and although we may try to linger over some scenes of the town or the countryside, we shall usually be aware that our picture cannot be complete, and that there may be no means of corroborating what we are told by our sources. While it is not possible to invite a reader to enter a Chinese home or farmyard of the period, I have tried to provide a series of views of those aspects of daily life on which the evidence casts light. How far such aspects should be regarded as normal and how quickly or slowly the situations that are described were subject to change in the four centuries of Han society are questions which must be left unanswered here.

For the sake of clarity it has sometimes been necessary to explain the growth of Chinese practice as this developed before the Han period; but such digressions have deliberately been kept to a minimum, and readers are warned when pre-Han or post-Han days are under discussion. Measurements are given in units of the metric system, and Chinese proper names, again restricted to a minimum, are rendered in the Wade-Giles system with the usual modifications. A short guide to further reading has been appended for the benefit of those who wish to study the subject in greater detail. I ask the indulgence of my professional colleagues for the simplifications and general statements that I have introduced, in the hope of bringing Han China to the attention of non-specialist readers in as clear a way as possible.

There are few scholars who specialise in Han studies to whom I am not indebted, but I would like to single out the following writers whose contributions have made it possible to embark on some of the topics discussed here: Cheng Te-k'un; Joseph Needham; Vivi Sylwan; William Willetts; and Yü Ying-shih.

Cambridge   M.L.

Contents

The Illustrations

The references given to the sources of the illustrations are not necessarily made to the original reports of the archaeologists. The following abbreviations are used:

a   *Hsin Chung-kuo ti k'ao-ku shou-huo* (Peking 1961)
b   *Han hua i-shu yen-chiu* (Shanghai 1955)
c   *Han-tai hui-hua hsüan-chi* (Peking 1955)
d   *I-nan ku hua-hsiang-shih mu fa-chüeh pao-kao* (Peking 1956)
e   Jung Keng, *Han chin wen lu* (Shanghai 1931)
f   *Kuang-chou ch'u-t'u Han-tai t'ao-wu* (Peking 1958)
g   *Kaogu*
h   *Lo-yang Shao-kou Han mu* (Peking 1959)
i   P'eng Hsin-wei, *Chung-kuo huo-pi shih* (Shanghai 1954)
j   R. Rudolph and Wen Yu, *Han Tomb Art of West China* (Berkeley and Los Angeles 1951)
k   *Ssu-ch'uan Han hua-hsiang-chuan hsüan-chi* (Peking 1957)
l   *Ssu-ch'uan Han-tai hua-hsiang-chuan t'a-p'ien* (Shanghai 1961)
m   Tsuen-hsuin Tsien, *Written on Bamboo and Silk* (Chicago 1962)
n   *Wang-tu Han mu pi-hua* (Peking 1955)
o   *Wen-wu*
p   *Wen-wu ching-hua*

Figure   **Page**

Figure   Page

Figure   Page

Figure   Page

Figure　　　　　　　　　　　　　　　　　　　　Page

Acknowledgement

The author and publishers wish to thank the following for their kind permission to reproduce the photographic illustrations included in this book:

The Trustees of the British Museum for figs. 5, 6 and 36
Musée Cernuschi and Editions Euros, Paris for fig. 62
The Chicago Natural History Museum for fig. 50
The National Museum, Copenhagen for fig. 78
The Freer Gallery of Art, Washington for fig. 11
Dr Joseph Needham and the Cambridge University Press for fig. 23
The Trustees of the Victoria and Albert Museum for figs. 1, 12, 13, 37, 60, 61 and 79

The thanks of the author and publishers are also due to the Executors of the late Arthur Waley and to Constable and Co. Ltd for their permission to quote the poems on pp. 89 and 151 from *170 Chinese Poems*.

I

The historical and
geographical context

The earliest traces of man's existence in China are the skeletal remains which are now known as 'Peking Man'. These pieces of bone are parts of at least forty-five individual men, women and children, and include five well-preserved skulls. They are thought to be about half a million years old, and there is reason to believe that Peking Man could already fashion tools of stone, control the use of fire and utter articulated speech. But he was still a very long way behind his followers who lived during various stages of the Old Stone Age (up to about 30,000 or 20,000 B.C.); or the more highly advanced human beings of the New Stone Age (from about 5000 B.C.) who had learnt to form and decorate pots for cooking and jars for storage, and to cut and polish stone implements of a markedly superior degree of sharpness and efficacy.

A radical change took place in the way of life in China when man first realised the properties of bronze (from about 1500 B.C.), and could equip himself with finer weapons and tools. For some time the use of the two materials continued side by side, and in the early stages the men who worked in bronze were quite ready to copy the forms and styles of the earthenware vessels of the New Stone Age. But the growing use of bronze with its finer qualities accelerated a tendency that had already started, for man to choose a settled rather than a nomadic form of existence. In addition bronze soon featured in the earliest evidences of a leisured civilisation in China, and of man's attention to matters that were not altogether intended to satisfy immediate material demands. In responding to those uncontrollable and unseen powers which might affect his

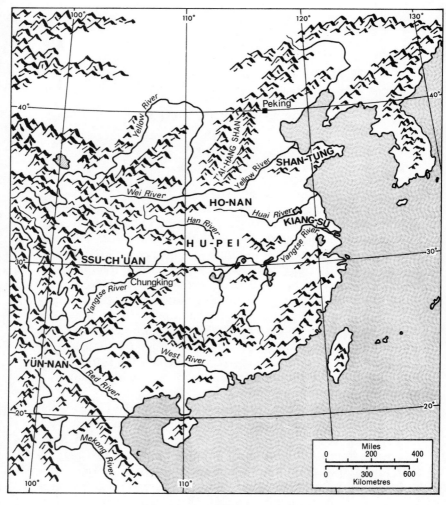

2 The physical features of China

(*The names of modern provinces which are mentioned in the text are shown in bold capitals*)

destiny, early man attended ceremonies, however crude, which required sacred spots or shrines for their performance; and the rites which were directed to appease the occult powers required precious items of equipment with which sacrifice could be made or libation poured. The highly ornate and beautiful bronze pieces made for these purposes became greatly treasured, and gave rise to some means of social or political organisation with which to ensure their protection. Such organisation soon led to the adoption of an hereditary form of leadership, or monarchy, and possibly to the maintenance of written records of administration. For a means of writing had appeared from about 1500 B.C. in one of the processes of divination, and the principles whereby written characters were being evolved then have governed the development of China's writing ever since.

Some of the most conspicuous traces of Chinese culture of the New Stone Age and the Bronze Age have been found at sites that lie along the valley of the Yellow River, and for this reason this area is sometimes described as the cradle of Chinese civilisation. But we also know of early cultures that arose in widely separate areas elsewhere in China, and whose styles bear certain unique characteristics. China should in fact be regarded as a sub-continent rather than as a single unified region, and this concept should be borne in mind when the developments of later ages are being assessed. For the area concerned is large and varied, comprising many different conditions of climate, terrain and soil, and harbouring the growth of peoples of different racial origins. Geographical conditions have been largely formed by the incidence of the mountain ranges that stretch out from Central Asia, and the main rivers which provide alike a means of transport, a supply of water and a cause of inundation.

The regionalism that has persisted in the last three thousand years of China's history can be seen most conspicuously in the variety of the sub-continent's natural products, whose growth has depended largely on rainfall. This varies widely from province to province, as might be expected in an area which extends for some 2000 kilometres from east to west and from north to south, comprising both sub-arctic and sub-tropical zones, and including a long sea-coast, high mountain ranges, isolated valleys and wide river basins. In very general terms rainfall is heavy in the south-eastern provinces, where the land catches the moisture that has gathered over the Pacific Ocean, and lighter in the hilly hinterland that lies on the fringes of Central Asia; and there is more rain in the lower part of the Yellow River Valley than in the higher ground that lies up-stream, west of the T'ai-hang hills and within the two great bends of the Yellow River. But the farmer's difficulties have usually arisen owing to the irregularity of the rainfall, as this often occurs in the limited period of the summer months. Con-servation may be far from easy, and the sudden onset of flood or drought is far from abnormal. Crop-failure or the virtual disappearance of farming settlements has never been rare in China.

Rainfall has largely governed the farmer's choice of his crops. While wheat, millet or barley have been best suited to the northern part of the sub-continent, rice has formed the staple food crop in the Lower Yangtze Valley, at least from the fourth century A.D. As very different techniques are required for the cultivation of these different crops, the farmer's needs in terms of irrigation, draught-animals and man-power vary consider-ably from province to province. Complex networks of water-channels may be needed for the cultivation of rice in the Lower Yangtze Valley; different techniques are needed to feed the fields that lie perched in terraces on the hills of Ssu-ch'uan; and the labour and skill of working the sandy silt of the north-west may depend less on the irrigation channel and more on the power of the traction ox. By intensive use of his land the farmer has eventually contrived to raise several crops in the same year; for example, in the far southern regions beyond the Yangtze River three rice-crops may sometimes be gathered annually; and in the Lower Yangtze Valley, once the rice has been harvested the dried fields are then used for wheat, beans or barley.

In addition to cereals, the Chinese peasant has raised hemp, which constituted the main source of textiles in general use until the introduction of cotton from the tenth or eleventh centuries A.D.; and he has kept mulberry-orchards on which silkworms have spun their threads for luxury apparel since at least 1000 B.C. Beans and other vegetables have been widely grown, together with various sources of vegetable oil and many kinds of fruit. Sugar-cane has been cultivated in the south-east; and since the third or fourth century A.D. tea bushes have been nurtured in the central Yangtze area and the coastal provinces of the south-east.

China's achievement of unity in this prevailing diversity of economic and geographical conditions is highly remarkable. Cultural unity has come about largely as a result of the general spread of the same system of writing; for the nature of that system is such that speakers of widely differing dialects have nonetheless been able to communicate with each other by means of the one form of the written language. At the same time cultural unity has still permitted the lively survival or practice of art forms and customs that are peculiar to certain localities or peoples, as can be seen by comparing the styles and products of different areas.

A second type of unity, that has been achieved in political organisation, has been no less remarkable, in view of the large number of persons concerned and the complex problems of governing wide expanses of territory before the advent of modern communications. Political unity has been achieved at various points of time in Chinese history, but it has not often lasted for more than a century or so; and the highest points of Chinese accomplishment have been reached with the coincidence or combination of effective leadership by the government

3 A decorative bronze plaque of two bulls, found at a site in the north-east of the Han empire. This may suggest cultural and racial exchanges between the Han Chinese and other peoples

4 A bronze ornament of two dancers found in the extreme south-west (modern Yün-nan province). Objects from this site show marked signs of a distinct local style and culture

and the active operation of the Chinese inventive genius and cultural skills.

These moments in history are best observed at a few points at which certain dynasties reached the height of their powers for a few decades, and historians have often concentrated on these occasions as illustrating the best gifts that China has offered to the peoples and civilisations of the world. However, such high points of achievement should not be regarded as being typical, normal or permanent. For each peak of successful attainment there is a corresponding moment of weakness in which government was slack rather than effective; when society was effete rather than vitalised; and when cultural initiative had given place to a stale adherence to obsolete forms. But whatever the strength or quality of leadership, the inhabitants of China have continued to pass their daily lives by practising their usual occupations as part of a dynamic and developing process. Cultural change, political maturity and the technological solutions of problems have come about as parts of a continued advance, that has not been halted by dynastic setback, moral corruption or foreign invasion.

Chinese history has usually been depicted in the political terms of a succession of dynasties, and it remains convenient to do so despite some misapprehensions, in order to provide a context for China's cultural development. From the beginning of the Bronze Age (*c.* 1500 B.C.) there arose a number of independent communities or kingdoms, and we know something of the material conditions and standard of civilisation of some of these settlements. As yet no single authority claimed universal rule over the sub-continent, and the term empire is inappropriate. But while some of these early communities were developing into kingdoms which possessed comparatively mature and complex forms of government, the daily lives of the population were being transformed basically by the developing use of iron in place of bronze. Although this major change started to gather momentum from about 600 B.C., the introduction of iron was gradual rather than sudden, and the use of the less hardy bronze implements and equipment continued simultaneously for some time. By the fifth and fourth centuries B.C. the use of iron wares was leaving its mark in Chinese society and government, by promoting the growth of industrial workings and communication lines, and stimulating the rise of cities. These changes in turn gave rise to the need for a more direct degree of political control and social organisation, and more intensive methods of government were soon being devised to satisfy the material demands of authority, such as the collection of taxes and the control of man-power.

A new epoch in China's government began with the formation of the first empire in 221 B.C. This was brought about by the efforts of one of the kingdoms (Ch'in) which had succeeded in taking over or annexing the lands of its six rivals. But although no other political authority existed which could challenge the claim of the first Ch'in emperor to rule, his dominion by no means covered the whole of the sub-continent, as there remained large areas where the officials of a central government could not yet be expected to operate effectively. In the two thousand years of imperial history that have ensued, there have been some 25 dynasties which have ruled over all or part of China, and whose authority has been acknowledged with greater or less obedience. Some of the dynasties have lasted for two or three centuries, some for a few decades; but

even the more permanent houses have not been able to exercise
fully authoritative control for the whole period of their existence. Some dynastic houses have been confined territorially,
e.g. to the northern or southern part of the sub-continent, with
the Yangtze River often acting as a division; and at these times
there have existed two or three houses simultaneously, all
claiming the natural right to rule the whole of China. For ever
since the days of the Ch'in and its immediate successor the Han
dynasties, centralised government has been the norm to which
emperors and statesmen have aspired; and it is in the light of
such ambitions that the plans of government, the activities of
individual subjects and the schemes of officials must be judged.

Man has evolved increasingly more complex and richer
forms of cultural existence throughout the two thousand years
of Chinese empires. The period can be divided in very general
terms at about A.D. 1200, when the cumulative effect of economic change, growing social organisation, intellectual experiment and cultural attainments was accompanied by a new
political maturity and a new relationship with China's neighbours. Hitherto China's empires had been based on the north-
west, where the capital city had been situated; after 1200 the
needs of the moment were such that the capital was now to be
situated in the north-east, usually at Peking. The first empires
had transported their supplies of food from east China to the
north-west, but from about A.D. 600 the north had grown to be
more dependent on the south; and from about 1200 the change
of emphasis was complete. This change in turn affected many
of the daily habits of the Chinese, leaving its mark on matters
of diet, housing and transport. A second major change, which
was to lead to the interruption of the Chinese tradition, can be
dated in the middle of the nineteenth century, when China
faced the western powers at a disadvantage. Military defeat,
dynastic decadence and the acceptance of western ideas have
since then led to China's rejection of her past sense of values
and to her establishment as a world power, resting on a completely different set of political and cultural assumptions.

In these processes the names of a few select dynastic houses
are often taken as symbols of different stages of China's progress, and the Han dynasty is often cited as the first successful
exponent of imperial government. The founder of the dynasty,

5 Door-way: pottery model, with designs impressed repeatedly. These include decorative scroll-work and the figures of guards (see the lintel and left column)

6 Well-head: pottery model, with tiled covering to shelter a pulley
(see figure *81*)

26

Liu Pang, bore the title of king from 206 B.C., and his kingdom lay in the western part of China. In 202 he assumed the title of emperor and claimed superior authority to govern the whole of the land. The imperial succession was maintained in the Liu family until its interruption by Wang Mang, who established his own dynasty in A.D. 9. However, this regime lasted only until 23, and in 25 the Liu house was restored to its position, which it retained until the final dissolution of Han imperial authority in 220. The period from 202 B.C. to A.D. 8, when the government was centred at Ch'ang-an, is usually known as that of the Western or Former Han dynasty; and that from 25 until 220, when Lo-yang acted as the capital city, as that of the Later or Eastern Han dynasty.

The Han period marks the first lengthy operation of imperial unity, in the sense of the continuity of a single dynastic house. It was a time of cultural dissemination and uniformity, in which many aspects of Chinese genius were fostered and brought to a flowering. Later dynasties were to look back to the Han period as a time of Chinese strength and resolution; and as the Han was regarded as the first of China's successful dynasties, the political forms and intellectual conclusions of the time have exercised a formative influence on succeeding dynasties. After the failure of the Han dynasty to maintain imperial government, China became subject to frequent incursions from the north, and for many years the northern part of the country was governed by non-Chinese emperors assisted by native Chinese officials.

It was in these centuries that the principal cultural import that China has ever received, the religion of the Buddha, took root; and by the time of the next effective establishment of centralised government under the T'ang emperors (from 618 to 906), the religion had formed an integral element in society and politics. Government was now more effective than it had ever been, even in the heyday of Han rule; cultural life was richer, with more frequent contacts with non-Chinese peoples, a more sophisticated view of literature, and the embellishment of many of China's arts and crafts. But although the T'ang period is often described as China's golden age, with its proliferation of poets and the establishment of court elegance, it was during the politically weak Sung dynasties (Northern

Sung 960–1126; Southern Sung 1127–1279) that the most brilliant aspects of the Chinese genius came to fruition, in the form of philosophical and intellectual initiative, technological creations, the exercise of critical appreciation and the enjoyment of a new standard of material luxuries.

Many historians recognise the emergence of a new type of Chinese society after the Sung period. The Ming (1368–1644) and Ch'ing (1644–1911) periods are known for the more forceful operation of imperial government, and the expansion of Chinese cultural influences in the cities of the Yangtze Valley and beyond. But despite some innovations that had come about imperceptibly, such as the merchant's rise to prominence in the towns, there were still many aspects of Chinese life which had been formed in the earliest days of imperial history and which still bore unmistakable marks of the societies of those remote days.

In the few pages which follow it would be impossible to do more than concentrate on a particular stage in the development of daily life in China, and whatever period were to be chosen for this purpose there would still be very large gaps in our knowledge. In the case of Han China it is possible to observe something of the daily activities which resulted from or were affected by the operation of government, and to indicate some of the problems which faced the men and women of the day, and the solutions that they reached. Owing to the shortage of information, it is not possible to describe the daily lives spent by the Chinese in their farms or hovels, in their palaces or courtyards; and we have perforce to be content with a mere glimpse at the application of government or technology to the everyday activities of the men, women and children of the Han age.

2

The emperor and his government

The Chinese system of emperor and government has proved to be one of man's most enduring creations. Since the establishment of the first of the empires in 221 B.C., the Chinese have developed a concept of government in which political responsibilities and social distinctions have been bound together formally, intimately and effectively. Society has consisted of men and women distinguished by the nature of their duties to one another, by the place they occupy in the structure of civil authority and by the degree of privileged treatment which they can expect to enjoy in an ordered state of administration. The concept has been evolved and supported by means of religious sanction, philosophical theory and the dire needs of practical government; and although the application of the concept has varied somewhat during the centuries and the distinctions of social groups have changed during the process, emperors, officials and subjects would normally have acknowledged that their situation in society and their well-being depended on a general acceptance of the same basic principles.

Emperor, officials and subjects form the broad groups in which Chinese society can be classified. Sometimes the concept is likened to a pyramid, in so far as the lower the ranks of society become, so do their members become the more numerous; and in so far as each layer, with the exception of that at the very top, both depends on its immediate superior and helps in its support. At the apex of the structure there stood the emperor, the unique source of temporal authority and leadership. He owed his position partly to his own merits and character, and, in theory, to the trust and responsibility implanted in him by a non-earthly authority, who was designated in Chinese thought and writing as 'Heaven'. The emperor was regarded as being the son of Heaven, and he was thought of as the intermediary of Heaven in its relationship with earth. The mandate bestowed by Heaven on its son conferred the right to expect obedience and loyalty from the inhabitants of the earth, and the power to preside over the authority that was needed for earth's government. But with this privilege the mandate coupled responsibility for the physical well-being and prosperity of the earth's inhabitants, and a readiness on the part of the incumbent to deport himself in a way that was worthy of the unique position that he occupied.

The tasks of government were carried out by the members of the next group in Chinese society, the officials, to whom the necessary authority had been delegated by the emperor. The officials were arranged in a series of ranks, whose number grew with the development of government; and from the earliest years of the Ch'in and Han empires officials were conscious of their positions in the hierarchy and the degree of dignity and status that was their due. Below the officials there lived the great mass of China's population, essentially the productive members of the community, whose occupations lay in China's fields and forests, in her lakes, rivers, and mines, in her highways and byways. Although the contacts between these elements and the upper reaches of society were rare and slight, their services were exacted with regularity and at times severity.

However highly the position of the emperor was in theory sublimated as being due to the ministrations of Heaven, account must be taken of the actual circumstances in which he or his forbears had succeeded in attaining that position. Many of the imperial houses of China were founded as a result of civil war or foreign invasion; and the mandate was by no means always conveyed from one member of a house to another without a series of quarrels or intrigues, conducted with some degree of violence or bloodshed.

At the time when the Han dynasty was founded (202 B.C.) there were officials and peasants in China, rich men and poor, orderly tillers of the fields and vagabonds, landowners and slaves. The Liu family, from which the Han emperors were drawn, did not derive from any particular class of society as this term is used today; for such distinctions did not operate at the beginning of the second century B.C. The founding emperor, Liu Pang, is sometimes described as being of peasant origins; as far as we know he was a man who had received no training in the gentle arts of Chinese culture, and the chance that led to his enthronement as emperor had come about partly by luck, partly thanks to his ability on the field of battle. As occurred on many subsequent occasions when a dynasty was founded, there had been a period of civil war in which the rival aspirants were gradually eliminated, and a single champion eventually survived to take command of his defeated rivals' resources. Once a man became established as an unchallenged victor and leader, he would legalise his position by acceding to his subjects' request that he would submit to enthronement as emperor; and in this way the mandate was 'conferred' on an incumbent who may have been unlettered, untrained and completely inexperienced in the tasks that lay before him. So it was with Liu Pang, on whom the mandate, with its duties, privileges and responsibilities, was formally bestowed in 202 B.C.

As soon as the Han dynasty was established, steps were taken to differentiate the emperor from other members of society; and as the emperors who succeeded the founder were nurtured in conditions specially created to enhance the dignity and authority of the imperial house they can be regarded as forming a separate element of the community. The distinction can be seen immediately in the arrangements made. for housing the emperor. He dwelt in the innermost part of a palace which was discreetly veiled from the prying eyes of an onlooker, protected from criminals and bandits, and secluded from the baneful influences of lowly or untoward inhabitants of the earth. Behind the walls that surrounded the palace buildings the emperor was attended by his servants and advisers, by his officials and his mentors. Entrance to the palace was by special gateways, guarded by watch-towers and sentinels; and the community that dwelt within the precincts included a host of women to attend to the emperor's needs; eunuchs to administer the palace and perform the necessary work within the women's apartments; courtiers to wait in daily attendance; and special members of the staff who looked after religious duties, prepared the emperor's food and medicines, or brought up the younger members of the family in the style to which their dignity was suited. The distinctive nature of the emperor's person was emphasised in most of his daily activities; in the long ceremonies of court or shrine over which he presided; in the prescribed robes which were duly prepared for each particular occasion; in the carriages and horses in which he made his progresses; and finally in the majestic mausoleum prepared for the time when 'ten thousand years and a thousand autumns would have passed away', and his mortal remains would be laid to rest with appropriate solemnity, luxury and security.

Before considering the officials (see Chapter 3) it is necessary to take a glance at the organs of government which they staffed. The system of the Han empire rested partly on the offices that had existed in China before the imperial age (i.e. before 221 B.C.). These had been modified to suit the needs and claims of the Han dynasty, but in the course of the four centuries of Han rule there came about a marked difference between the theoretical and prescribed authority of the principal offices of state and the actual powers exercised by certain bodies or dignitaries at court. However, the structure rested throughout on the acknowledged derivation of authority from the emperor and its transmission from one official to his subordinate through a complex hierarchy of departments and offices.

The basic structure comprised government in two parts: the offices of the central administration that were situated at the capital city and the provincial organs that lay scattered throughout the empire; and the relationship between the two parts was such that it was undisturbed by changes in the territorial extent of the empire. Thus at times of expansion further provincial units could be set up in an attempt to control newly penetrated regions; and at times of retrenchment these could be withdrawn in the face of enemy activity without affecting the main administration. In the later centuries after the Han period, when dynastic rivals had established several regimes simultaneously, each one could attempt to control his part of China by applying the same system of government to his empire.

The officials of the central government of Han China were

7 A head-rest made of jade. It was found in a tomb which may be that of a Han king who received charge of his kingdom in 54 and died in A.D. 90

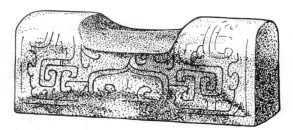

generally responsible for consulting with the emperor and determining major policy decisions with him or on his behalf; with devising means to collect revenue; and with maintaining order inside China and security from menaces without. A few posts in the central government that were of a consultative nature only were restricted to elder statesmen. But the main responsibilities rested with two very senior officials who corresponded very approximately with modern dignitaries such as a prime minister and a head of the civil service. These two officials enjoyed the closest contacts with the emperor, and it was through their agency that acts of government were promulgated. They received reports from junior officials and brought them to the emperor's attention when they deemed it necessary to do so. They issued decrees which the emperor signed and which provided for the implementation of his decisions; for in name all decisions were taken by the emperor in person.

Below these senior officials there existed nine major offices of state, or ministries, whose functions were concerned partly with the operation of government and partly with the maintenance of the imperial establishment. Their responsibilities included: religious ceremonial, observation of the stars, record keeping; superintendence of the court and imperial household; security of the palace and control of its guards; care of the imperial stables; administration of punishments for crime; receipt of homage and tribute from foreign leaders; maintenance of records of the imperial family and regulation of the degrees of precedence for its members; collection of state revenues and direction of working projects; and charge of the imperial purse and disbursements therefrom.

These nine major offices or departments of state were

organised under the direction of a single senior official assisted by a number of subordinates, and the specialist duties were divided between a number of constituent bureaus or sections. For example, the Grand Controller of Agriculture was responsible for collecting revenues of state, which were partly delivered in grain, and for directing working projects. He was assisted by deputies who supervised work such as the upkeep of state granaries; the maintenance of stable prices of basic commodities; or arrangements to facilitate the transport of the bulky and perishable consignments of grain to areas where it was most needed. The Keeper of the Imperial Purse, who collected certain dues in coin, was supported by a whole series of junior officials engaged in tasks such as the preparation of the emblems and badges needed by officials, or supervision of the craftsmen who designed and fashioned the luxurious furnishings and equipment of the palace.

There were also other, less senior, agencies staffed by officials of the central government, and in most cases they were likewise occupied in the written work of civil servants rather than in tasks of executive administration that involved direct contact with the inhabitants. There was also provision for senior military posts such as General of the Left or the Right, or General of the Van or the Rear, whose incumbents possessed the same rank of seniority as those highly placed officials who were in charge of the nine major departments of the central government. These latter posts were filled regularly; as soon as a vacancy occurred, through death, dismissal or retirement, another official was named to fill it, and we are fortunate enough to possess a fairly complete list of the names of those who held these senior posts from 206 B.C. to A.D. 5. For the General officers, however, appointments were by no means so regular, as it was not always necessary or desirable to keep the establishment at full strength.

The provincial government of the Han empire was organised in two types of administrative unit which were termed commanderies and kingdoms. At the outset of the dynasty the empire comprised a total of 15 commanderies and 10 kingdoms. But after about a hundred years some of the kingdoms had been eliminated, reduced in size or split into several smaller kingdoms. As a result the number of commanderies had

34

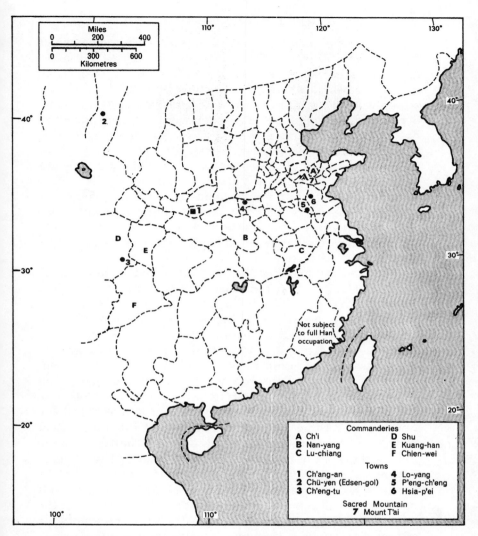

Commanderies

A Ch'i	D Shu
B Nan-yang	E Kuang-han
C Lu-chiang	F Chien-wei

Towns

1 Ch'ang-an	4 Lo-yang
2 Chü-yen (Edsen-gol)	5 P'eng-ch'eng
3 Ch'eng-tu	6 Hsia-p'ei

Sacred Mountain
7 Mount T'ai

8 The administrative divisions of Han China, A.D. 1–2. The divisions shown as dotted lines between the 83 commanderies and 20 kingdoms of A.D. 1–2, should be regarded as approximate only, and allowance should be made for areas which, though nominally included in a commandery, were not necessarily subject to the full exercise of Han authority. For the north and north-west, divisions cannot always be shown between areas that were open to both Han and non-Chinese penetration

increased considerably, and this was further augmented by the establishment of new commanderies in the many directions where territorial expansion had taken place. Thus, in A.D. 1–2, which is a year for which we possess a full list of the administrative units of the empire, there existed 83 commanderies and 20 kingdoms. The commanderies were governed by Grand Administrators who were appointed by the central government, and the kingdoms were entrusted to kings. These were near kinsmen of the emperor, and in theory a king was succeeded on his death by his son. In practice the central government took a hand in manipulating the succession of the kings; and in any event it was the central government which came to appoint the senior assistants of the kings. As a result, the kingdoms were hardly less directly controlled by the centre than the commanderies.

Commanderies and kingdoms were alike divided into smaller constituent units which are usually termed prefectures. In all there were 1587 prefectures in A.D. 1–2, each one being of approximately the size of an English county. The prefectures were themselves divided into districts, and the districts were further subdivided into wards. Officials responsible for the various tasks of government were stationed in their different degrees of importance in prefectures, districts and wards; and in many cases the appointments to these locally held posts were made by provincial rather than the central authorities. Some aspects of government could be delegated to the minor, local officials of the districts or the wards, who shared with the prefects the work of implementing the decisions of the central government, and of bringing the Chinese face to face with the demands and encroachments of temporal rule. Local officials set about the collection of tax in grain, textiles or cash from the farms or the villages; constables of the districts were responsible for arresting criminals, deserters or fugitives from justice, or any villager who gave shelter to such law-breakers. Local officials were responsible for calling up the emperor's subjects to serve their allotted time in the labour gangs or the armed forces; and the prefects or their subordinates maintained granaries, canals and roads in a proper state of repair. Finally, the provincial and local authorities were responsible for the upkeep of a system of communications, without which no government could operate effectively. Urgent despatches and routine mail were carried from one post to another on horseback or by runner; and officials of the central government or the provincial agencies could ride at speed from one commandery to the next by means of the chain of stations and post-horses that were carefully kept for their use.

3

The officials

Many Chinese statesmen and writers have been glad and proud to describe the institutions of their empire, and a picture of a highly complex structure of offices emerges from their writings. Although we shall never know how closely such an idealised picture corresponded with the actual practices of state, it is clear that from the Han period onwards imperial governments have tried to establish a civil service which could organise many of the activities of the emperor's subjects; and from the earliest days of the Chinese empires the government has been faced with the problem of finding the necessary number of educated and local men, to whom the grave responsibilities of administration could be entrusted, but who would not yield to the temptation of abusing their positions so as to serve their own interests.

The difficulties of recruitment and training were solved gradually over the course of many centuries in a way that has moulded some of the characteristic features of Chinese society. The official was needed by governments and he was in short supply; his position therefore became enhanced and he gained a prestige that for long remained unmatched in other sections of the community. Recognition of the civil servant's value, arrangements to educate him, and provision for his steady advance from a junior to a senior post have combined to stress distinctions of grade and privilege, and there have always been material and external forms whereby this hierarchy was made visible. 'Officials are the leaders of the populace', ran an edict of 144 B.C., 'and it is right and proper that the carriages they ride in and the robes that they wear should correspond to the degrees of their dignity.' Emblems of office in fact varied according to grade in a series of golden, silver and bronze seals, decked with purple, blue, yellow or black ribbons according to an official's position and salary.

Since the fifth century B.C., philosophers had been advising that the highest offices of state should be given to men who were distinguished by virtue of their abilities, rather than by the circumstances of their birth; and ability was regarded as comprising both moral integrity and intellectual capacity. This principle remained in favour among intellectuals during the Han and later imperial periods, but, although most governments claimed that they supported it, practice was often tempered by considerations of circumstance or expediency. Nevertheless the ideal concept of the official affected his education as this gradually developed; for this usually comprised a means of inculcating moral principles as well as training the intellect, and took account of the fine achievements of successful governments of the past. There are also some suggestions of a prejudice against the employment of men of wealth or commercial interests in office, for fear that rich men who lacked the necessary qualities would be able to buy their way into the service. Although these fears were sometimes realised, there is perhaps less significance in these precautionary views than is sometimes suggested.

From the outset of the Han period attempts were made to recruit suitable candidates to serve in the offices of state. In an edict of 196 B.C., senior officials of the commanderies and the kingdoms were ordered to send men of promise to the capital city, where their talents could be considered and suitable appointments made. A century later it had become a regular annual event for each commandery or kingdom to send up a few candidates for the same purpose, and by the middle of the first century A.D. a quota had been fixed. Thus, for every 200,000 inhabitants in his commandery a governor was entitled to submit one candidate who had been chosen for his proven moral standards and devotion to family duties, and between six and ten men who were believed to possess more than a nodding acquaintance with literature; and by A.D. 140 a total of at least 200 candidates of the first type were presenting themselves each year for inspection, drawn from the interior parts of China.

On arrival at the capital city the men were subjected to some form of examination or selective process. This was usually conducted by senior civil servants, but there were occasions when the emperor himself addressed questions to the men and judged their answers. However, little is known regarding the procedure for examination, the topics chosen for questioning, or the form, verbal or written, in which the answers were presented. A valuable fragment of the Han laws refers to the practice of testing youths aged 17 for proficiency at certain types of reading and writing; and the histories record cases of a number of officials whose careers started when they were awarded a first, second or third class in their initial tests of selection.

In theory this road to an official career lay open to men from all stations in society. Indeed, it is said that a famous official who sponsored the cause of education in about 120 B.C. had himself tended pigs at a time when his family's fortunes had been at a low ebb; but his qualities were such that he ended his career as the emperor's principal adviser of state. There are also many cases of men who rose to positions of eminence after a youth spent in the countryside or at provincial towns; but there is little doubt that proximity to the central government itself, or good family connections, played a highly important part in easing the path towards advancement. Despite the ideal concepts mentioned above, officials could often recommend their sons to fill vacancies in the service, and some few posts may have been held on an hereditary basis. Or else, a girl whose charms had captivated an emperor could secure positions for her kinsmen that were suitably honourable and lucrative. We also know of occasions when a man successfully purchased the title of an office for ready cash. The bargain in such cases was well worth while; for an initial outlay the purchaser acquired a salary, the respect of his fellow-men and certain highly valuable social and legal privileges. These included exemption from some of the harsher forms of conscript service, and favourable treatment should he infringe the laws and be liable to punishment by the state.

When a candidate had been duly presented from the provinces, or by one of the officials of the central government, and had been accepted as possessing the necessary powers of

9 An official, wearing robes and a sword and carrying a writing tablet. This painting, in black, scarlet and blue on a yellow background, dates from A.D. 182, and was found on the wall of a tomb in the modern province of Ho-pei

intellect, he joined a pool of gentlemen waiting at court in expectation of assignment to a vacancy. Sometimes there may have been as many as a thousand men standing by in this way, and their services were useful as supernumerary advisers or as courtiers. When a vacancy occurred, a new official was appointed, at first in a probationary capacity; if he was found wanting, he could be removed from the post; alternatively, his appointment could be confirmed as permanent after a year's trial. There were also various types of temporary appointment.

A further feature of the traditional Chinese civil service which can be traced to the Han period is seen in the periodic reports which were made on an official during his service. Every three years the provincial authorities were obliged to submit reports and accounts covering their area of responsibility, and the evidence which was submitted included reports on the performance of junior officials. Probably these gradings were couched in stylised categories by means of short formulae; and there was little scope for original or independent comment on a man's character, or on exceptional ways in which he had rendered services or failed to discharge his duties. There is some evidence to suggest that these reports included the name and position of the official; an assessment of his services simply as 'high', 'medium' or 'low'; a note of the length of time spent in the office in question; a certificate of his ability to read, write, manage accounts, and of his cognisance with the laws; his height and age; and the distance that separated his native home from the office where he was serving. This last detail acted as a certificate that there was no infringement of the rule which banned a man from serving in his home district. The rule was presumably introduced as a safeguard against corruption, but it probably did not operate for the more senior officials. These periodic reports were sometimes followed by promotion or demotion.

Posts in the civil service, whether in the central or the provincial government, were graded according to stipend. These were described in terms of an annual allowance of measures of grain, ranging from the grade of Full 2000 to 100. Actually officials were paid partly in grain and partly in coin, and sometimes in bolts of silk; and it is impossible to suggest the real value that the stipends commanded. Usually a man was promoted from one grade to its immediate superior, and this sometimes happened automatically after the completion of a given period of service. There were also some exceptionally gifted or fortunate officials who were permitted to jump several places up the ladder, thanks to an imperial edict. Demotion or dismissal occurred after proven dereliction of duty or incompetence, or in cases of indictment for crime. Officials were allowed one day of rest in five and were entitled to an allowance of sick leave. When a man retired honourably from a post on account of old age, he may have been lucky enough to receive special bounties of money or textiles. Sometimes a pension was granted, and in one case we hear of this being specified for life, at the rate of one third of the stipend earned by the official in his last post.

In Han China, as in later dynastic periods, a single group of individuals formed the empire's scholars, civil servants and statesmen. Candidates for office were trained in the first place to be scholars rather than administrators. A man could rise from the low and rather scorned ranks of the provincial service to enter the offices of the central government; and if he eventually became head of one of the nine departments, or held one of the two more senior posts, he would find himself engaged in duties that were very different from those of the humdrum life of a clerk or provincial civil servant. He would now be associated with formulating policies and taking administrative decisions that might be of far-reaching importance throughout the empire. And members of the profession were proud of their situation. They were respected by other members of society as forming one of the highest elements in the community; in their progress along the hierarchies of office they had probably acquired reasonably large material possessions, either in money or in land; and above all they were the acknowledged leaders of society, and set the pace of cultural achievement for the rest of China. Within their own ranks they observed strict rules of protocol which regulated their behaviour towards one another, the styles whereby they addressed their senior or junior colleagues, the formulae in which their written communications were framed, and the degree of precedence which they took in various activities of public life.

The more junior officials, in both the central and the provincial administration, conducted most of their work in their offices, where they received reports from their colleagues; interviewed members of the public; drafted reports on their work; pronounced judgment in cases that were brought for arbitration; completed their records of taxation duly levied; or prepared suggestions for submission to their superiors. Outwardly their offices may have differed little from the residences of prominent townsmen, built with imposing gateways, spacious courtyards and shaded apartments. These were laid out symmetrically, so that when a visitor was escorted to the presence of the great man, he could hardly fail to be impressed with the dignity of his way of life and the formality of his surroundings. And this effect was no mere accident; it was deliberately contrived so as to remind the public of the privileges as well as the duties that accompanied the service. Each official had his ordered place in society and in the service of his emperor; and while his servants or slaves freed him from the menial tasks of living, he in turn acted as the underling of his own superiors in the service.

Eventually, perhaps, a man was promoted to one of those high positions which required attendance at imperial audiences, and on these occasions strict rules of court governed the

10 A teacher and his pupils: the teacher is protected by a canopy, and the pupils carry their
text-books in their hands; one has a scholar's knife
tied behind him

proceedings. Senior officials made their way to the palace
carried aloft in carriages of the style to which they were entitled. They must arrive at the designated gate of the palace at
the appointed time, attired in their proper robes and head-
dress, with their seals and ribbons of office. Here they would
dismount and the remainder of the journey to the imperial
presence was made on foot, but at the double; and in this way
the servant of state demonstrated his zest for his task and his
determination to serve his emperor to his best ability. In special
cases of privilege extended to elderly statesmen the rule was
relaxed, so that a venerable figure could proceed calmly to the
audience hall and arrive there in a suitable state of dignity and
composure.

The quality of Han official society varied greatly during the
400 years of the dynasty's duration. There were times when the
ideals of integrity yielded place to corruption, and when the
few favoured families near the throne were able to sponsor the
appointment of clients whose abilities were yet to be tested.

Opportunities for highly placed officials to exploit their positions were by no means unknown. On one occasion, in about 80 B.C., the government had a building project which involved the removal of a large quantity of sand and gravel, and it was necessary to hire privately owned ox-carts to carry 30,000 loads. The treasury decided to pay a price of 1000 coins for each load, but a highly placed official managed to increase the price paid to 2000, and netted a cool profit of thirty million coins. There are also accounts of the high-handed way in which provincial governors were sometimes able to behave towards the local population of their commanderies. But however authoritative or arbitrary they might be, their dispensation was often preferable to the violence or lawlessness that might ensue in the absence of an official administration, when a strong local family could impose its will on a defenceless population by the use of hired gangs of armed supporters. And for every example of corruption that is recorded the histories bear witness to the opposite case, of an official who completed his work with scrupulous honesty and conscientious devotion to duty.

Schools existed for one purpose, that of training future members of the civil service, and they were attended mostly by sons of officials or other highly placed families. The formal establishment of a recognised institution of learning in the capital city can be traced to a suggestion that was made by a senior official in about 120 B.C. The purpose was to provide recruits for the service, and due stress was laid on the value of proven intellectual powers as a qualification needed for appointment. At times there was a regular complement of pupils who could be accommodated at this institution, and a quota of men who were to be passed with a first, second or third class degree. There were also some forward-looking officials who hoped to set up similar means of education in the provinces, for the same purpose. Some provincial officials took care to select young boys of promise and sent them to be educated at the capital city, Ch'ang-an (from 202 B.C. to A.D. 8) or Lo-yang (from A.D. 25 to 220). In time these young men would return to their native farms, villages or towns, there to earn the respect and perhaps the envy of their boyhood friends; for they had gone out as playmates, whose untutored rustic speech was little different

45

from that of their companions of youth; but they now came back with the full glory of official authority and the polished speech and mannerisms of the metropolitan world.

We also know of the growth of private establishments during the Han period. Sometimes a seminary arose around the figure of a well-known scholar, whose expert profession of a particular school of thought attracted pupils or disciples. We are told that these were sometimes to be numbered by the hundred; and some of the famous statesmen of the Han period received their training and formed their opinions in this way.

Ideally the Chinese liked to think that schooling began at the age of eight, but it is unlikely that such practice was regular. The first accomplishment that a pupil needed was the art of reading and writing, and he must have spent many hours in mastering the forms of written characters (see Chapter 7). To help with this task Chinese scholars or school-teachers compiled word-lists, and at the end of the Western Han period the imperial library included about a dozen of these works in its collection. Parts of the lists have survived, and it can be seen that they formed catalogues of characters which denoted objects of the same category, e.g. house, dwelling, cottage, habitation, storeyed-building, reception room, hall.

These lists also helped pupils when they came to their next task, that of mastering the texts of the classical or scriptural writings. These included works of prose and poetry, some of which were believed to have been compiled or edited by Confucius (? 551–479 B.C.). Some of the texts were indeed considerably earlier, and they were valued for their moral teachings and their accounts of traditional statecraft. There were also certain other works of more recent composition, which laid down the rules of behaviour for social and political occasions, for the guidance of sovereign and official, for the older and younger members of the family. An intimate knowledge of these writings was indispensable to anyone who pretended to an education.

Some teachers concentrated on giving their pupils a piecemeal, literal commentary on the classical texts, without worrying unduly about their general meaning or the message that was being imparted. Others may have taken a more liberal view of the needs of education and tried to expound the real

11 Incense burner, of bronze, with gold, silver, turquoise and carnelian inlay. The design includes twelve mountain peaks, with scenes of human and animal figures; dated in the Western Han period or possibly earlier

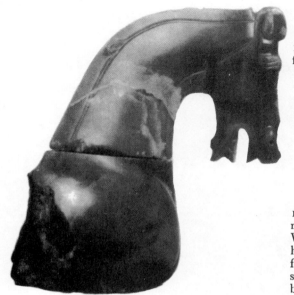

12 Horse's head: jade figure

13 Mastiff: model in red earthenware. While this type of harness was retained for dogs, it was superseded by the use of breast-straps on horses (see figure 71)

48

significance of the master's words. Sometimes the dry records of ancient history were amplified by anecdote or reference to historical fact; or a teacher might be tempted to explain an early text in the terms of contemporary religious practice or superstitious belief.

At some stage in their training pupils were introduced to mathematics. They learnt something of theory and something of practice and many of the exercises that they were given were related to everyday affairs. Some of the examples could be provided with modern counterparts:*

A fast horse and a slow horse set out together on the 3000 *li* [i.e. 900 kilometres] long journey from Ch'ang-an to Ch'i. The first day the fast horse travels 193 *li*, thereafter increasing his speed by 13 *li* each day. The slow horse covers 97 *li* on the first day, thereafter reducing his speed by $\frac{1}{2}$ *li* each day. After reaching Ch'i the fast horse starts his return journey and meets the slow horse. When does the meeting take place and how far has each horse travelled?

or

A man is hired as a salt porter. If he is paid 40 cash for carrying two measures of salt for a distance of 100 *li*, how much will he be paid for carrying 1.73 measures for a distance of 80 *li*?

Fig. 14 may serve to clarify a well-known theorem; although the figure is reproduced from a printed edition of the eighteenth century, the textbook of which it formed part was originally compiled in about 50 B.C.

Education was regarded as a means of improving the human character, of correcting a man's faults and repressing his more ignoble motives. At the same time it was a means of fostering human talent and of enabling pupils to improve and exploit the natural faculties with which they had been endowed. There are no specific descriptions of educational theory or practice of the Han period, but we know of at least one sixth-century writer who believed expressly in the principle of 'spare the rod, spoil the child'.

* The answers thoughtfully provided in the textbook are as follows: (1) after $15\frac{135}{191}$ days; the fast horse has travelled $4534\frac{46}{191}$ *li*, and the slow horse $1465\frac{145}{191}$ *li*. (2) $27\frac{11}{50}$ cash.

Many of the statesmen and officials who rose to power in Han China did so by the normal way of nomination or recommendation. They then served in a junior capacity in the provinces, or perhaps the central government, and may finally have achieved appointment to one of the major responsible positions of state. There were also those whose careers were not crowned with such conspicuous success, but whose contributions to the Chinese way of life was no less remarkable and no less permanent. To conclude this brief account of the government and officials, let us consider the situation at the top in about 90 B.C. As it followed some alarming incidents brought about by intrigue and plot the situation was abnormal or even critical; and the actual control of government was by no means as regular as the institutions of the empire prescribed.

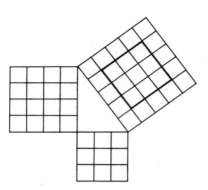

14 A figure for a geometrical theorem. From an eighteenth-century print of a Han text-book

First we must take note of a man called T'ien T'ien-ch'iu. He was descended from the famous T'ien family which had occupied the throne of Ch'i, in east China, before that kingdom had been incorporated into the newly emerging Ch'in empire (i.e. shortly before 221 B.C.). In 91 B.C. there had been an abortive attempt to manipulate the imperial succession. Fighting had broken out in Ch'ang-an city, and there had been a large number of casualties. As a result of the incident the empress and the crown prince were forced to commit suicide, but the faction which had launched the plot was soon discredited and its rivals restored to power. By expressing his opinion that the crown prince had been the victim of a miscarriage of justice, T'ien T'ien-ch'iu succeeded in ingratiating himself with the emperor. He was appointed to one of the senior posts in the government, and bore responsibility for what we should term foreign affairs, and which in fact included negotiation with the leaders of non-Chinese tribes and maintenance of the correct protocol (i.e. the presentation of suitable gifts to the throne, use of the correct formulae in communications to the Han emperor etc.). In the next year (87 B.C.) he was appointed chancellor, the most senior of all posts in the service. He had had no previous experience as an official and no achievements to his name; nor could he boast of any outstanding talents. A Chinese envoy who was serving at the time on a mission in Central Asia found himself acutely embarrassed when his hosts asked him to explain why the appointment had been made.

But to anyone who understood the political situation then prevailing at Ch'ang-an the reason would have been fairly obvious; T'ien was simply a figure-head. Although the chancellor was nominally head of the government, actual administrative power lay in the hands of a triumvirate composed of Huo Kuang, Sang Hung-yang and Chin Mi-ti; and it evidently suited these three men to preserve the correct forms and institutions, while making sure that the men nominated to the highest offices were political nonentities. The three men themselves came of very different backgrounds.

Huo Kuang's half-brother Huo Ch'ü-ping had been a famous general, serving his emperor with the utmost success until his death in 117 B.C.; and he had also been a nephew of the very empress who had been driven to suicide in 91 B.C. Huo Kuang had in the meantime served at court in various inconspicuous capacities, and for about 20 years he had acted as a past-master of circumspection in that somewhat dangerous situation. In the last days of the ageing emperor Wu ti (died 87 B.C.) the question of the imperial succession arose. Huo Kuang found himself charged with the task of implementing the imperial will, and acting as head of a regency which was to guide the footsteps of the young emperor; in this task he was to be assisted by Chin Mi-ti and Sang Hung-yang.

The new emperor, Chao ti, was aged eight at his accession (87 B.C.), and Huo Kuang found himself dictator. Of his close collaborators, Chin Mi-ti was a member of one of the leading families of Central Asiatic tribesmen. On an earlier occasion his father had refused to surrender to a show of Han force, with

15 An earthenware jar painted in scarlet and blue on a white background

the result that the family had been taken into Han custody. Chin Mi-ti was aged 14 at the time and had been put to work as a groom in the palace stables (121 B.C.). At a display of the imperial horses that was held in Wu ti's presence, Chin Mi-ti was the only attendant who was too proud to acknowledge the presence of majesty; and his behaviour and fine appearance earned him the emperor's respect and admiration. The incident was shortly followed by an appointment to an official post and the enjoyment of Wu ti's personal friendship and substantial bounties.

The position of a foreigner at the Han court can hardly have been easy and the increasingly generous privileges bestowed on Chin Mi-ti naturally excited criticism and antagonism. But his conduct and loyalty remained beyond reproach, and he took care to refuse some of the highest favours which he was offered in view of the jealousies that they might arouse. His son was married to one of Huo Kuang's daughters, and he assisted in the regency for a year before succumbing to a fatal illness.

The third member of the triumvirate is in many ways the most interesting to the historian. Sang Hung-yang came from a business family of Lo-yang, and his contributions to the welfare of the Han empire had been made some 30 years before Wu ti's death and the regency. We first hear of him as an attendant at court in about 140 B.C., at the tender age of 13. The precocious youngster had evidently earned himself a reputation for his skill at mental arithmetic, and he was soon taking part in the councils of a few commercial and industrial experts who had a voice in the affairs of state. Sang Hung-yang saw the value of applying the methods of business to the problems of government, and, when his turn came to hold high office, he introduced a number of bold and imaginative measures that were designed to control the distribution of China's natural resources, with greater efficiency and profit to the authorities.

At the time of Wu ti's last illness Sang Hung-yang was the senior statesman responsible for agricultural production and the collection of taxes. We may perhaps surmise that, although his resolute policies and obvious strength of character may not have endeared him to his colleagues or rivals, he was too powerful a figure to exclude from the highest councils of state; and his participation in the regency is not surprising. The open rivalry and hatred which seems to have existed between Sang Hung-yang and Huo Kuang was brought to a head in 80 B.C., when Sang was involved in an unsuccessful plot against the throne; and he died a traitor's death at the hands of the executioner.

4

Social distinctions
and occupations

Very broadly the Han population was divided into officials and non-officials, with the latter element greatly outnumbering the former. The non-official groups included a great variety of individual types, and both here and among officials there were other distinctions that were perhaps of a less formal nature but of equally important practical consideration. These were the differences brought about by circumstances of birth or the possession of wealth; by the type of occupation and the recognised status that a man enjoyed in society.

Family relationships played a vitally important part in the growth of Chinese society, culture, and religion during the pre-imperial age (i.e. before 221 B.C.), and have continued to exercise a dominating influence over certain aspects of Chinese civilisation ever since. Membership of the same clan or family had constituted the earliest form of group relationship to be recognised. It had implied participation in commonly accepted religious rites, agreed obedience to the same authority and acceptance of its leadership; and from such beginnings there had arisen the earliest forms of political organisation in China. With the growing sophistication of government that resulted first in the formation of kingdoms (from about 500 B.C.) and later a single empire (221 B.C.), considerations other than those of birth began to take a predominant place in social developments, and ultimately resulted in the emergence of an official class. But in the Han period there still lingered more than a vestige of the privileges that had been attached to birth, to membership of a prominent family with its inherited wealth, respect and natural authority. The imperial family itself perhaps sought to consolidate its unique position in society by upholding these distinctions; and while the system of centralised government was still being evolved and there were still insufficient trained officials for imperial administration, the government relied on the respect commanded by certain families and their authority, as a means of sharing responsibility for its work.

From about 100 B.C. trained officials were coming forward in greater numbers and the importance of birth was yielding place to that of merit and ability. Indeed, although there existed means for powerful statesmen or senior civil servants to promote their sons' advancement, these opportunities were resting less on descent from a family of ancient lineage and more on claims to have served the emperor with loyalty and efficiency.

While the importance of birth within a prominent family was decreasing, that of wealth and its inheritance was growing. The fifth and fourth centuries B.C. had witnessed the more general circulation of coin, the development of communications, commerce and cities, and the accumulation of fortunes by a few rising merchant families. By the Han period society had reached a higher point of material sophistication, and as the demand for manufactured or rare commodities became more insistent, so did the opportunities for the shopman, businessman or wholesaler become more attractive. Although the great age of Chinese mercantile activity was not to begin for some thousand years or more, even in these early centuries the wealthy merchant occupied a place in society that was by no means negligible.

Perhaps the most important and valuable form of wealth lay in arable land, and for its means of acquisition we must turn again to the fifth and fourth centuries B.C., before the imperial age. The growth of trade at that time had been one of the factors which gave rise to the recognised exchange of arable land for cash; and, despite the unsettled political conditions of the next few centuries, it had become possible and even desirable for rich families to invest their wealth in real property. Some of the estates owned by these *nouveaux riches* families had grown to very large proportions, and some may have survived into the Han period. Certainly during the

16 At a banquet the participants knelt on mats with
stands for the dishes in front of them. An attendant
waited on each side of a guest

second century B.C. it was possible for rich men to build up
considerable land-holdings, and a famous statesman of those
days drew a sad and bitter contrast between such vast resources
and the lot of many a peasant, who had not sufficient land on
which to stand an awl.

Between these two extremes there grew up a great variety of
types of land-holder or worker, encompassing the small-holder
who could yet afford to live on the work of others; the farmer-
cultivator, who worked shoulder to shoulder with his wife and
children in the fields; the tenant who held land by lease from
the large estate owner or the government; and the wage-earning
peasant or labourer. Unfortunately there is no evidence with
which to estimate the proportionate numbers of these widely
different members of Han society, but the general assumption
that the great majority of the Han population was engaged in
tilling the land is not to be gainsaid. Other occupations of the

generally unprivileged population of the Han countryside included forestry and the exploitation of mines, lakes and rivers; and many men were doubtless employed in working irrigational devices and other mechanical aids to farming (see pp. 174f).

By the Han period individuals were known by their family surname and a personal name which was chosen at birth; and while the number of surnames was comparatively small, considerable variety could be introduced in selecting the right expression for the personal name given to a child. Many personal names consisted of a single term, but some comprised two written characters and contrived to convey a message or prayer, such as *Yen-nien* or 'Protracted years'. In the higher ranks of society a man could later be given a secondary style by which he could be known, and this usually alluded to some incident in his past. Part of the importance in possessing a name lay in the need for identification in the government's registers whose uses will be described below (see pp. 62, 69). In describing an individual it was usual for the surname to be written before the given name.

Apart from distinctions of birth, wealth and occupation, Han society was marked by differences of status and its attendant degree of privilege. Imperial government was based on the concept of rewarding meritorious services and punishing those whose actions were detrimental to the state; and rewards took the form of distinctions or orders of rank which were bestowed by imperial edict. There were in all twenty of these orders; the highest, which is usually designated as that of 'marquis' was hereditary, and marquises took precedence over all other members of society except for those few kinsmen of the emperor who had been appointed as kings to govern certain territories (see p. 36). The highest 12 of the 20 orders were bestowed on officials only; and although orders could be accumulated by an individual with each successive bestowal, a bar prevented non-officials from rising higher than the eighth order.

The higher the order that a man held the greater were his privileges likely to be. At the lower end of the scale these did not count for much; but with the gradual increase of status a man acquired a greater degree of preferential treatment from the officials, or became entitled to a less severe degree of punishment by law. At the top of the hierarchy the marquisates carried the right and responsibility for levying taxation over a specified number of households. Although most of these dues had to be forwarded to the government, marquises enjoyed the receipt of some income directly from the lands over which they had been granted these rights.

If a man who held orders of rank was found guilty of a crime he could be punished by deprivation of some or all of his orders, and he would then revert to the commoner status of the greater part of the population. Below commoners there were several types of individual whose status was regarded as substandard. There were the convicts sentenced to a maximum term of five years' labour, and put to work by the local authorities. Sometimes convicts were kept bound in irons; but they could be raised from their despised status by direct amnesty of the emperor. These were granted at irregular intervals, at some periods in almost every year. Alternatively convicts were sometimes given partial freedom, whereby their status was advanced but they continued as members of a hard labour force for a definite period of time.

Han society also included slaves, who probably never amounted to more than one per cent of the population. Originally these were the male and female relatives of convicted criminals who had been 'confiscated' by the government along with their other goods. Such persons were first put at the disposal of the offices of state, and it was only when there was a surplus that the government would be willing to sell them to wealthy members of the public. In times of acute economic distress a peasant would try to sell his children into slavery for ready cash. While slaves were forced to obey the commands of their masters and were counted as their property, the slave-owner's rights were by no means unlimited, and certainly did not include arbitrary powers of life and death. By contrast with convicts, slaves normally retained their status without amelioration throughout their lives.

Slaves who were in private ownership were employed on a number of duties. There was general work for them to do in running a household, looking after the kitchen and attending to other menial tasks. Sometimes they acted as bodyguards for their masters, and they could be called upon to wait on master or mistress for personal or intimate duties. If they were skilled, they could be trained as acrobats, jugglers or musicians; they were trusted with confidential work, such as that involved in business undertakings, or with the religious duty of guarding ancestral graves and tending the surrounding grounds. Some slaves were probably put to work on the land, but it is unlikely that this practice was very widespread, and Han agriculture can in no way be said to have depended on slave-labour. On the home estates of the large land-owners slaves were employed in making domestic utensils, weaving textiles or in market-gardening; and they may sometimes have been formed into gangs of armed retainers, sent by their masters to perform acts of violence or oppression.

For the slaves who were held in official hands there was probably a similar mixture of skilled and confidential duties with the work of unskilled labour, and there was some criticism of the failure of government offices to make full use of the slaves put at their disposal. Slaves worked in the palaces or offices as messengers, door-keepers or attendants at banquets. At court they kept watch on the water-clock and tolled the hours on the drum; and in the imperial parks they were sometimes sent to look after dogs or horses, or the domesticated and wild beasts with which the stables and grounds were stocked. In addition, official slaves may have been employed on the heavy work of cartage and

17 Figure of an entertainer, found in a grave in Ssu-ch'uan

59

haulage, of loading and towing barges up the rivers, on which so much of the cities' well-being and material existence depended.

Most members of the population worked as China's peasants, distinguished, if they were fortunate, by up to eight of the lower orders of rank. But these orders carried no exemption from the statutory obligations to the state, which included an annual period of service in the government's labour corps. For this reason many a peasant must have found himself working from time to time as a transport man on the rivers or canals; as a miner in the state-owned iron and salt mines; as a road-builder preparing highways for the emperor's progress; or on any other project that authority deemed necessary. The peasant was unconnected by birth with the houses of the great, and he rarely possessed resources on which he could call. For much of the Han period he existed in a state of uncertainty, often in conditions of distress or penury. For he lived at the mercy of nature, as often as not the victim of flood or drought, which could destroy his livelihood at a blow. He could easily be reduced to selling his meagre tools or draught oxen, if these had survived the poor fare of a hard winter, or an outbreak of plague; and he would have little spare cash with which to buy the seed for the next year's harvest.

Possibly he could borrow money from a neighbouring great land-owner; and if, when the time came for repayment, he had already disposed of his goods and his animals, and sold his children into slavery, then his land would pass into the possession of his creditor, and he would stay to work another man's soil for a small profit, on terms which he had no power to question. Small wonder that many of the peasants were forced by economic stress to take to a life of the wilds, living as vagabonds or beggars, as starvelings or robbers. These were the men who could easily be attracted to join the ranks of a rebel or bandit leader, whose brave promises of paradise on earth rang sweeter to the ear than the official's demands for his tax, or a creditor's insistence on his dues.

Economic need also determined the size of the peasant's family who lived together in the same house or hovel, and conditions varied considerably from time to time and place to place. Probably we shall not be far wrong if we bear in mind a

18 Guardian figure: from the door of a tomb, with ring and animal-face clasp to indicate the handle. The robed guardian carries a sword and a weapon mounted on a long pole

farming household of four to five members, representing two or three generations. As there was no room for non-productive members, it would seem unlikely that a farmer could practise concubinage, but for the wealthy ranks of society the picture is somewhat different. At the start of her married life a wife would take her female attendants or servants with her, or she might be accompanied by a younger sister or relative. These and others might fill the role of concubines, being released from such duties in due course and rendered free for marriage. Convention or written prescription dictated the number of concubines which was permissible at the top of the social scale, with the emperor's establishment comprising 14 grades, each one being suitably distinguished by title and rank.

There were many domestic tasks in the palace that were more suitably entrusted to women than to male courtiers, and which naturally fell to the concubines to perform. As their position was by no means derogatory, the term concubine is perhaps somewhat misleading. The greater the household, the more numerous the tasks for these girls and women to undertake, and the maintenance of large establishments by the wealthier households need not necessarily have been due to reasons of prestige. A further consideration, whose importance grew as a family rose in the social scale, was the need to provide an heir to inherit the family's possessions and responsibilities. For the emperor it was a matter of supreme importance that there should be a suitable candidate to receive Heaven's mandate on the demise of the crown. Infant mortality was frequent, and the man on whom final responsibility rested for earthly blessings could afford to run no risks in this respect. In some cases the existence of numerous concubines in the palace led to political intrigue and domestic complications; and it was generally regarded as essential to discriminate sharply between the legal heir and his mother, and the other children that the emperor sired.

Thanks to the registers of the inhabitants which local officials compiled at regular intervals, and thanks to the fortunate inclusion of two specimen sets of figures in the Chinese histories, we possess census counts for the years A.D. 1–2 and 140. There is no means of checking the accuracy of the returns, which clearly depended on the efficiency and honesty of the officials; but the figures cover all the provincial units of the empire, and their internal consistency supports the claim that they are reasonably reliable. However, while they may well cover the numbers of households and individuals with whom the officials were actually able to make contact, they cannot cover that large multitude of fugitive or semi-assimilated inhabitants of the hills, woods and marshlands who were virtually inaccessible to the Han official. The figures that are given follow:*

| A.D. 1–2 | 12,233,062 households | 59,594,978 individuals |
| 140 | 9,698,630 households | 49,150,220 individuals |

One of the reasons why the second set of figures are lower than the first is that in 140 some parts of north China were subject to the incursion of non-Chinese tribesmen, and the officials were not able to make the necessary returns. It can be calculated that the registered household of these years included, on average, between four and five members; and the total counts may be compared for interest with an estimate for the popula-

* The figures given here are as they appear in the histories, but in view of faulty addition there they should be corrected to something in the order of 12·4 and 57·7 million (for A.D. 1–2) and 9·5 and 48 million (140).

tion of the Roman empire at the time of Augustus (27 B.C.–A.D. 14) of between 70 and 90 million.†

The figures in the Han histories are given separately for each provincial unit, and it is possible to see in very general terms how unevenly the population was spread in the different parts of China. The region of greatest density was that of the Yellow River Valley, with more localised dense regions in the north-west, where the capital and other cities lay, and the Upper Yangtze Valley (the modern province of Ssu-ch'uan). At the time of the earlier census there had been comparatively little penetration by the Han official south of the Yangtze River, but it is possible that this had become more intense during the 140 years that separated the two counts.

† Michael Grant, *The World of Rome* (Mentor Books, 1960, p. 47). This figure breaks down to 30–50 million in Europe, with perhaps the same number or rather fewer in Asia and something short of 20 million in Africa.

5

The force
of government

As envisaged by many Han statesmen, paradise on earth spelt a state of peace and plenty, of general contentment in the countryside and of little interference by authority in the daily lives of the inhabitants. Certainly, a government needed to possess powers of leadership and even coercion, but these should be exercised as lightly as possible. Public works should be reduced to a minimum, so that the population would be left to pursue its own work of growing its crops without interruption. At its best government would be effortless and the population free of problems; all ranks of society would enjoy a state of affluence and preserve a healthy respect for law and order.

This ideal state contrasts sharply with the conditions that are described in protests levelled against some of the Han governments. Some of these were composed in highly critical and sophisticated terms, analysing the causes of economic distress and decrying the flight of people from the Spartan life of the farms to the glorious opportunities for money-making in the towns. A statesman who lived in the last half of the first century B.C. listed seven factors in an attempt to explain popular disaffection. These included the imbalance of the natural world, which resulted in flood or drought, and thence in harvest failures; the implication here was that such disasters were little less than the warnings of a superhuman authority of the shortcomings of the emperor's government and of the need for moral reformation. Other reasons for contemporary distress could be traced directly to human activities, such as the government's excessive demand for service in the labour corps; the endless exaction of taxes by greedy officials; the insatiable appetites of the great houses for material goods; or the continual demands for military service, which denied a man the chance to carry out his seasonal tasks in the fields. Finally, government itself was ineffective, and the continual alarms that fell upon the ear told their own tale of civil disorder and robbery.

The actual situation probably varied considerably between these two extremes, according to the efficiency of the government, the integrity of the officials and the quality of the harvest. The Han age witnessed the growing complexity of Chinese society; the intensification of the government's will to govern; and the call for a higher degree of cooperation between man and his neighbour, in the interests of a richer and better organised form of existence. In such circumstances no government could hope to realise the early ideal of a rule which relied on precept without interfering in the daily lives of the population; and one of the permanent achievements of the Han emperors was the foundation of normal and regular means of bringing authority to bear on their subjects.

Decisions of government were promulgated in the first instance by edicts signed by the emperor. These were published by the central authorities and passed from one office to its subordinate, until the necessary action was taken. Edicts covered all types of subject and activity, such as the nomination of an imperial concubine as empress and her son as the crown prince; provisions for religious observances; arrangements for taxation or provincial administration; the encouragement of agricultural work; the initiation of building projects, repairs to river dykes or schemes to improve communications; the regulation of relations with foreign leaders; or the bestowal of privileges on an individual or of bounties to the general public.

Some imperial bounties were extended fairly generally. For example, the gift of an order of rank was at times made to one principal male member in each household, and these orders were on occasion accompanied by a distribution of wine or meat. Sometimes a bounty took the form of an amnesty for criminals, with the addition of gifts of money or silk to other, more respectable members of the community according to their status or official post. Bounties were sometimes given on occasions of state, such as the nomination of a crown prince, or his

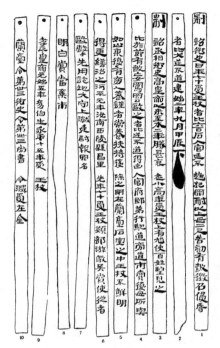

19 An imperial decree of bounty, conferring privileges on seventy-year-old men of certain status. The strips, found in a grave in north-west China, measure 1 Han foot (23 cm.) in length

attainment of majority. This event occurred on reaching the age of puberty which was variously set between fourteen and twenty; and it was celebrated by the ceremony of first donning the cap of manhood. There were also times when a general bestowal of imperial favours was limited to a particular area, such as one affected by natural disasters, or a region which had lately suffered the expense and trouble, albeit the honour, of forming the scene of an imperial progress. Perhaps the best of all these gifts was that of exemption from taxation, as this affected each family directly.

Imperial favours were sometimes granted to a particular individual or his family. This was an obvious and easy means of rewarding an official for his services; and in the case of a man who had lost his life in pursuit of his duties his descendants might benefit from the gold or cash that he was posthumously given. When an official received a marquisate in this way, this honour would in time pass to his son, together with its valuable privileges and responsibilities. Alternatively, recognition of services

66

could take the form of granting a man's family exemption from obligations to the state. A further type of edict conferred privileges by virtue of a man's age or blameless record; and we are fortunate enough to possess a contemporary copy of just such an order, which had been reverently laid on the coffin of the beneficiary (fig. 19).

The permanent provisions of Han government were framed in the form of Statutes or Ordinances. These general directions for the conduct of the administration and the control of the population were of universal application, and it is possible that copies were compiled from time to time and distributed to provincial authorities for information and action. Unfortunately no such complete document still exists, and it is not even possible to estimate its original size or the number of its provisions. From surviving quotations we know some of their titles, such as the Statutes on 'Robbery', 'Banditry', 'Gold and Coins'; or the Ordinances concerning 'Palace Guards', 'Official Ranks' or 'Ritual Fasts'. Other Ordinances provided for matters such as the care of the aged, or irrigation and agriculture; and while many were known by their titles, some were evidently set out in series such as Ordinance A, Ordinance B, etc.

On the lowest level of the administration, local officials relied on persuasive as well as legal powers to preserve law and order in their areas. Most parties to disputes would probably prefer compromise or unofficial arbitration to official processes which might be incomprehensible, and the force of custom was probably very strong in the more remote country districts. A traditional respect for the guidance of village elders was perhaps as deeply rooted as the acceptance of the need to obey the commands of the emperor or his representative.

But the officials of government had to take a hand in cases of disregard of the Statutes or the Ordinances. Although no exhaustive list remains of the crimes for which these laws prescribed regular punishment, some can be identified, e.g. infringement of imperial majesty, such as reviling the emperor, entering the palace precincts without authority, or using that part of the main road which was reserved for imperial passage; interference with the processes of government, such as forging official documents or acceptance of bribes; or violent acts which would upset civil discipline, such as murder, assault and injury, extortion, robbery or banditry. Adultery and incest were punishable in some cases, as was failure to denounce a criminal to the authorities.

Once a man was accused of committing a crime he was arrested and detained in prison, sometimes in manacles. An official interrogation followed, in which the lash may have been used to make sure that the truth was being revealed. Sometimes the force of the flogging was so severe that a man died in prison; and at least one official realised that the practice, so far from bringing out the truth, would just as well encourage a man to lie, as a means of escaping from his predicament. Witnesses were called to give evidence, and if necessary they too might be detained in prison, so as to ensure that they would be present at the trial. Finally, when statements and written evidence, if such were available, had been taken into consideration, an account of the charge was read out to the accused, together with his own assertions; and if he felt that he was being treated unjustly he could request a further enquiry. Finally he would be sentenced to a punishment that fitted the crime. The death penalty was carried out by beheading, or cutting in two at the waist; and in extreme cases not only was the criminal himself executed, but members of his family were exterminated with him. Sometimes criminals were punished by mutilation, such as tattooing, amputation of the nose or the feet, or castration; or, in lighter cases, by shaving the beard and whiskers. In addition there would be sentences to hard labour; and the more exalted members of society could be punished by exile, monetary fines or by a ban on holding an official position. This somewhat rigorous conduct of justice was sometimes relaxed for charitable reasons. For example, the very old, or pregnant women were treated more leniently than others. Privileged members of society could ransom themselves from severe punishment or mitigate its worst excesses by means of payment or by rendering meritorious service.

The basic instruments with which officials could control the population and its work were the registers of the land and the households, which were usually compiled once a year. Reference has been made above (see p. 62) to the use of these lists in indicating the extent of China's population, but the principal

20 The carriage of a medium grade official, with an axe and two lances. Sometimes these vehicles were accompanied by runners carrying banners

reason for their compilation was to facilitate the regular and efficient collection of the taxes. The land registers showed the holdings that were vested in a man's name, together with a very broad classification of its quality, in one of three grades. This information was necessary for the procedure of collecting the land-tax, which was usually assessed at the standard rate of one thirtieth of the produce. However, the calculation of the amount due was no straightforward matter. It would have been a tedious process if the officials had to make the necessary calculation each year, in exact proportion to the season's yield; but it would have been highly unjust and impractical to assume that there had been an even yield throughout the empire and to levy tax accordingly, whatever the crop that had been sown. As neither of these methods was suitable, one of three standard assessments was probably made, in accordance with the classification of the land as good, medium or poor; and the registers included the information that was required to levy the appropriate rate.

Land-tax was charged to the landlord, whether he was an owner of a great estate or an owner-cultivator. Tenant-farmers did not pay land-tax to the officials, as this charge was met by their landlord. He in his turn would exact corresponding dues from his tenants; and instead of paying at the rate of one thirtieth of their produce to the state, tenant-farmers may sometimes have had to pay a rent of a half or even more of their yield to their landlord.

The registers of households enabled officials to call up those who were liable for service and to collect the poll-tax, which constituted the other primary source of state revenue. Generally speaking this was levied at the rate of 120 coins per head of the adult population, and 23 coins for each child aged between seven and 14. Other rates were payable for slaves, and the tax was usually paid in coin. Although no examples survive of the entries made on the household registers, it is likely that they included a note of the name, sex, relationship and status (i.e. order of honour, if any) of each member of the household.

By the eighth or ninth month of each year the local officials had assembled the information needed for these registers, and it was then ready for submission as a report to the central government. Such reports may have included the full details or they may have been no more than a summary; they were delivered from the commanderies every year, except for the more distant areas, whence they were sent every third year. Of the two copies that were usually presented to the central government, one was supposedly perused by the emperor, and the second was examined in the equivalent of the prime minister's office. By this means the central government could exercise some check on the conduct and integrity of its provincial officials, and gain some idea of the empire's resources of territory and man-power.

Brief reference has been made above (p. 60) to the statutory obligation of males to render one month's service annually in the state's labour corps, and the registers of households were one of the means of ensuring that all those who were liable for this service were actually being called up. The duty started at the age of 23, or for one period 20, and ended at 56, but those with nine or more orders of rank to their credit were exempt. It was also possible in certain circumstances to pay for a substitute to perform the work, but it is unlikely that this practice was widespread. Theoretically these arrangements could provide the government with a labour force that was about one million strong, but it is extremely unlikely that all those who were liable were always called up or that such a figure was ever reached.

The men were employed in building projects and government industries, and in keeping the lines of communication in a good state of repair. Building projects included not only the palaces of residence for the emperor or members of his family, but also the majestic mausolea which were prepared for their entombment. The care with which this work was supervised can be judged from a set of inscribed stones that were probably hewn for the tomb of the emperor An ti (reigned A.D. 107–25). Each one is inscribed with its specified dimensions; with the serial number of its position in the structure; and the date when it was examined and passed by the inspecting officials. It is possible and even likely that the stones were cut by conscript labour.

Industrial undertakings on which the *corvée* men were occupied were largely the iron, copper and salt mines and their manufactures (including the mint). Convicts were employed on the same work by the supervisory agencies of the government; and according to an estimate of about 50 B.C., which may have been somewhat exaggerated, a total of over 100,000 working days were spent annually in the iron and copper industries.

The transport of grain presented difficult problems to a government which wished to keep its population supplied with life's necessities. The natural communication lines of China are somewhat limited, as the waterways are not always suitable and the mountain ranges act as barriers which separate one province from another. Moreover, the principal grain-producing area of the north-east lay at some distance from the capital city and the other towns that had arisen in the west. Similarly the forces who were stationed to guard China's northern frontier were in no position to grow all their own supplies of food, even if the climate and the terrain had favoured such projects, and the daily rations had to be brought from elsewhere to feed the chain of outposts that stretched into Central Asia.

However, the transport of grain was not a lucrative source of profit to a merchant adventurer; grain is bulky and easily perishable, and China is no natural breeding ground for pack-animals. If merchants did undertake to arrange deliveries to the distant frontiers, they had to be rewarded, usually with the much coveted orders of rank. It is likely that it was left to the local officials and conscript labour to complete the laborious

21 A view of the San-men Gorge, from east to west. This series of islets lay mid-stream in the Yellow River, some 250 kilometres east of Ch'ang-an and seriously obstructed the passage of supplies to the city (see p. 158)

tasks of humping the grain by hand or ox-cart over land; of loading the tubs or sacks for passage up the Yellow River; of trans-shipping it where necessary, and carrying it, where rivers or canals allowed a passage, to points whence it could be unloaded for its final destination.

The Han governments were well aware of the difficulties and expenditure involved. About 55 B.C. we hear of the figure of 60,000 servicemen who had been employed on taking four million measures of grain by water to supply the capital city, and of plans to reduce this burden. On some occasions canals were dug, either to ease transport or to improve irrigation and make the area more self-supporting. Conscript and perhaps convict labour was likewise employed on this work, as well as on that of road-making where this was more suitable. An inscription which was cut to record the exploits of certain local officials in south-west China informs us that in A.D. 63 a force of 2,690 convicts was engaged in building a road in the precipitous country of those regions. As part of the work 633 timbers were erected to support five bridges, and the total number of man-power days spent was 766,800. If the complete force of 2,690 men had been engaged continuously, this task would have been completed in some 285 working days. Unfortunately the original stone has been broken at the point where the inscription accounts for the materials used in the project, and these cannot be determined fully; the text does refer to the use of 369,84– tiles.

Conscript labour was also used in engineering works and attempts to control floods. In 109 B.C. the emperor personally supervised the repair of a major breach in the banks of the Yellow River which had been damaging the surrounding countryside and disrupting farmwork for some 20 years. The histories record that tens of thousands of conscripts were involved, and that His Majesty encouraged the men by reciting a poem of his own composition while the work was in progress. Material evidence of work that was perhaps undertaken by state labour has recently been found at a site in the modern province of An-hui. This was intended both to conserve water in times of shortage and to prevent floods during heavy rainfall. The site has been tentatively associated with the direction of Wang Ching, a famous water engineer who was appointed to be a provincial governor in A.D. 82.

Wang Ching came from one of the Han colonial settlements in Korea, where a remote ancestor had migrated so as to avoid implication in the dynastic intrigues of the first quarter of the second century B.C. His father had served in a local capacity, and had found occasion to prove his loyalty to the Han house in A.D. 30. As a boy, Wang Ching had read widely, and showed a marked inclination towards the sciences of the heavens, mathematics and technological problems. In about A.D. 60 his name was put forward as an expert water engineer, and he was soon able to show his mettle in a successful project to control flooding, in which he applied his own system of dykes.

In 69 he was asked to advise in connection with the Yellow River. A number of attempts had been made in the preceding century and a half to forestall the danger of flooding, principally by directing the main flow of water into several outlets leading to the sea. However, maintenance of the dykes had been neglected for some decades, largely owing to civil war and administrative difficulties, with the result that the Yellow River now encompassed the sites where the water-gates had once stood, and the surrounding area suffered considerably. Wang Ching evidently impressed the court with his appreciation of the problems and his recommendations. He was provided with such records as the government possessed and the necessary material resources, and a large force of conscript labour was put at his disposal. He then set about the work; he rebuilt the dykes, and made a topographical survey. His men cut tunnels through the hills, cleared the obstacles that lay amid stream or diverted its course; and a series of gates which he established at regular intervals served to regulate the flow of the water and to prevent inundation. Careful as Wang Ching was in his use of man-power, the labour involved was still enormous; and when the emperor inspected the completed project in the following year, he gave orders that a regular complement of officials should be posted to maintain the installations.

Wang Ching's reputation was now made, and both he and his associates in the work were rewarded by promotion or appointments in the public service. In 72 he accompanied the emperor on a tour of inspection, and was again rewarded for his conspicuously impressive achievements. As a regional inspector of a large area in east China, he intervened in a political argument, to prevent a scheme for moving the centre of government back from Lo-yang to Ch'ang-an, where it had been established during the Western Han period.

Wang Ching's final post was that of provincial governor of Lu-chiang, a commandery that stood on the north bank of the Yangtze River, west of the modern city of Nanking. The area was somewhat undeveloped at this time; the art of ploughing with oxen was not yet practised, and despite its potential resources the land was not self-sufficient. Long ago some attempts had been made at irrigation, and Wang Ching soon contrived both to put these schemes into order, and to direct the working efforts of officials and local inhabitants so as to make the area productive. With the ox-drawn plough whose use he now enjoined, many plots of virgin soil were reclaimed, and a new era of prosperity dawned. In addition the governor promulgated a respect for law and order and arranged for the cultivation of the silk-worm and production of silk. His civilising influence, as we are told, was felt throughout the area.

Wang Ching died while still in office. He had always had a profound interest in omens and prognostications and in their value in determining day-to-day activities; but unfortunately his book on the subject has long since disappeared.

6

The army

In addition to their duties in the labour corps, able-bodied males were required to serve in the armed forces, probably for a period of two years, at some time between the ages of 23 (or for a short period 20) and 56. The age-limits were thus the same as those for the obligatory service in the labour corps, and the men were also liable for recall at times of emergency. The statutory two years' service was probably spent in a variety of ways; part of the time may have been passed under training, and part in units that were stationed inside China. There was also the onerous duty of serving in the garrison forces that were established permanently at some of the frontiers, but it is not clear whether this obligation formed part of the statutory two years' service or whether it was additional. Most of the information regarding military service derives from administrative records that were made by the garrison forces of the extreme north-western part of the Han empire.

It is not possible to estimate the potential strength of the Han conscript army with accuracy. If the call-up was maintained efficiently for the full period of two years, the total number of men in service at a given time could conceivably have amounted to a million, but it is extremely unlikely that the forces ever approached that figure. While final responsibility for military matters devolved on the governors of the commanderies, for the Western Han period there was an establishment of military commandants in each commandery who organised the arrangements for conscription, and these posts survived into the Eastern Han period in the remote commanderies of the frontiers. Provincial officials could call on men to serve in times of emergency such as banditry or invasion, and in the north of China the system could be utilised so as to maintain the static garrisons permanently. Generally speaking the provincial authorities elsewhere did not maintain large regular forces; and if the central government decided to authorise a governor to call out troops for a specified purpose, the commission to do so was duly conveyed in writing, together with an emblem or tally which ensured that the orders had not been fabricated.

Most of the conscripts served their time as infantrymen, but there are some references to the use of troops carried in galleons and presumably used in coastal waters or in the river systems of the south. Service in the cavalry was probably voluntary, and may have been associated with those privileged members of society who were not liable to conscription, or with the unassimilated horsemen of Central Asia. Conscript soldiers received basic rations of food, clothing, and equipment, but no pay.

For special military ventures the government nominated an experienced campaigner to be a general officer, and the title that he bore sometimes included a reference to his task or to the area where he was to lead his troops. If the operation was thought to be of minor importance, a junior officer, or colonel, was appointed, but in each case the government would provide specific instructions to provincial authorities, ordering them to put a requisite number of men at the officer's disposal. Sometimes a general officer's force would be made up of contingents from several parts of China, and might comprise infantry, cavalry (from the commanderies at the borders) and some convicts; and if engineering works were likely to be involved, some of the men might be drafted from the labour corps.

For very large-scale campaigns it might be necessary to nominate several general officers and one commander-in-chief. Such campaigns were fought at times of strength and prosperity, and it is evident that the generals could choose their own methods of conducting their business and controlling their troops. Thus very different styles were adopted by Li Kuang and Ch'eng Pu-chih, who held commands at the northern frontier in about 140 B.C. The two generals each disposed of

22 Guards: from a fresco (black, with some red, on beige) in a tomb situated in the north-eastern part of the Han empire

23 Watch-tower: remains of fortifications built as a protection against intruders from Central Asia; from the north-west of the Han empire

task forces with orders to seek out and defeat the enemy tribesmen of Central Asia. Li Kuang proceeded with the smallest possible degree of formal organisation, and would encamp wherever he chanced on suitable supplies and pasture. He had his men take their ease, without bothering to arrange a system of regular sentry duties; and he saw to it that the written work of his headquarters was reduced to a minimum. Ch'eng Pu-chih, however, was an officer of a very different type, who insisted on the maintenance of regular formations and on routine sentry and guard duties. His officers were kept busy at their written work until dawn, and his troops had no time for relaxation. Both generals had their moments of success; the historian drily observes that the enemy feared Li Kuang more than Ch'eng Pu-chih, and that there was no question which general was the men's favourite.

Although foreign policy was at times dictated by the needs of defence and retrenchment, a general attempt at expansion led Chinese forces deep into Central Asia on several occasions. From about 120 B.C. the government was encouraging the growth of trading activities in these areas. Elsewhere it was extending the scope of the Han official in the uncharted and proverbially unhealthy regions south of the Yangtze River, or in the south-western recesses of the modern Yün-nan; and at the same time a policy of colonial expansion was being developed in Korea. These ventures were never maintained for long with sufficient strength, and the difficulties of communications and supply brought several campaigns to a standstill. Nevertheless due credit must be given to the Chinese willingness to plan large-scale expansionist ventures, and to attempt the difficult task of arranging a rendez-vous by different armies before embarking on joint operations against an enemy.

The commandants who controlled the static defences of the north organised their forces with a principal headquarters which worked directly to three or four companies. These consisted of perhaps thirty sections, of an officer and some four to ten men each. While the military operations of the sections were controlled by an intermediate command post, or platoon headquarters, for administrative purposes the sections worked straight to the company commanders. There are many references in the Chinese histories to the strength of the forces who

24 A battle with fallen enemy and charging horseman

were engaged in various campaigns, but those figures are probably exaggerated and unreliable. For the static defences, it can be estimated very tentatively that the line of posts that lay between Shuo-fang and Tun-huang commanderies could be manned by some 3500 servicemen, including officers; but this figure must be increased to account for the men who served behind the lines, and it throws no light on the problem of estimating the actual number of servicemen engaged in the fighting expeditions launched for expansionist purposes.

Chinese historians have not usually paused to describe the battles fought by Chinese troops, but sometimes a painting or sculptured relief was made to illustrate a feat of arms. The account of a battle which follows probably derives not from the pen of an eye-witness, but from a description of a series of pictures, doubtless idealised, that were presented to the court and shown to the ladies of the palace. It concerns an episode in the fighting between the Chinese and Chih Chih, leader of one of the Central Asian communities with whom the Chinese had long been at enmity.

In 36 B.C. a Chinese expedition had reached the outskirts of Chih Chih's walled headquarters and proceeded to lay siege to the site which was probably situated at approximately 71°E, 43°N. The Han forces could see their foe displaying his many-coloured banners on the walls, at whose foot a troop of cavalry was exercising. On either side of the city gate there were infantry practising their drill in very close formation. Challenge after challenge rang out from the walls, and some hundred enemy horse galloped towards the Chinese camp, to be driven off by heavy cross-bow shooting. The Han commanders followed up this slight success by attacking the enemy horse and foot that were posted outside the city, actually forcing them to withdraw inside; and the drums were now beaten for a general advance by Han troops. Each section had been allotted its sector, to ensure that all outlets from the city were blocked. The van was formed by heavy shieldsmen, and these were followed immediately by the spearmen and cross-bowmen, whose arrows forced the enemy to withdraw from the turrets and battlements of the main wall. However, there was a double palisade of wood that lay outside the fortifications, and the enemy could use this as a cover from which they could shoot at the Chinese, until the latter succeeded in setting it on fire. Night fell, and the enemy made a vain attempt at a sortie. Chih Chih now took a personal part in the battle, appearing in full armour on the walls, accompanied by a large number of his womenfolk, whose bows were trained on the Chinese. But a Han arrow soon found its target, wounding Chih Chih on the nose; and many of his womenfolk were killed. Forced to leave the walls, Chih Chih seized a horse and galloped into the city to call for reinforcements.

It was now past midnight, and the surviving enemy soldiers who had managed to hold out in the outer ditches were forced to withdraw within. They now climbed the walls and started shouting; and their cries were answered by a large force of Sogdians who tried in vain to relieve the city. By dawn, fires had broken out on all sides, and the Chinese had driven off the relieving force, with a great tumult of bells and drums. They now prepared for the final assault, pressing forward with their large shields and launching a concerted attack on the city. Chih Chih and his close associates fled into the palace, which was then set on fire; and as the Han officers and men jostled each other to force their way inside, Chih Chih was stabbed to death.

Our knowledge of the life of the conscript soldier depends on the evidence of fragments of administrative documents which have been found during the last half century in the extreme north-western part of the Han empire. Following the initiation of a positive policy to extend China's trading activities, from about 120 B.C., the lines of defence that had been erected in the

25 Reconstruction to show a cross-bowman in action

north and which formed China's first 'Great Wall' were extended westward into Central Asia, so as to form protected routes of communication, for the passage of a merchant and his caravan, or a diplomat with his retinue. The protection of these lines devolved on the Han forces, which consisted for the greater part of conscripts.

These were the men who had been called up with their fellows from China's villages and towns, and who had set out on the six or eight weeks' march to their destination from the Yellow River area, the fertile valleys, the forests and the terraced farms of the Upper Yangtze, and many other regions where the recruiting officers were performing their duties with zeal and efficiency. The men were probably marched to the frontier in their own groups, and could thus enjoy each other's company on the way. Probably they had little understanding of the conditions that would soon face them. Indeed, as they looked around them on their march, their hearts must have been stirred or dismayed by unfamiliar sights; by landscapes of an awesome nature; precipices waiting to trap a man at the slightest stumble; stretches of land which no amount of irrigation could render fertile; or forests which surely concealed evil spirits or wild beasts, ready alike to prey on the unwary passer-by.

When the men eventually reached the area of the 'Wall' they had already passed through changes of climate; and some of them may have been prepared for the arduous extremes of the north-west, where tropical heat raged in the summer, to be followed by the bitter cold of the winter months. The further the conscripts were led the more difficult the terrain had become; there were now few spots where nature unaided would allow a farmer to raise his millet or barley. The local inhabitants, if indeed the troops had seen any during the last stages of their journey, lived a different life from that of the Han Chinese, relying partly on growing crops and partly on stock-breeding or hunting for their livelihood. The mounted groups whom the conscripts may have sighted in the distance were probably of non-Chinese stock, with different bodily features and dress, and speaking a completely different language from their own.

When at last they arrived at the headquarters of the military commandant the new recruits were assigned for service where they were most needed. There was a variety of work to be done in the static defence lines; but most of the men would probably be sent either to the small units guarding the watch-towers or to the farming settlements that had been specially established by authority, and which were supported by irrigational works and man-power with which to wrest a crop from an uncharitable land. The commandant's staff knew from their records where the men were most needed; and having arranged where they were to be drafted, they sent them to the stores to draw the necessary clothing and weapons.

Some of the military units or squads were stationed forward of the main defence lines, but for the most part they were occupied in garrison duties in the square watch-towers, which had been built within sight of each other and linked by means of a high earthwork. The towers were mainly constructed of brick, covered with a coating of plaster and whitewash. Some of them boasted several rooms, whose doors were fitted with bolts to secure privacy. Some towers rose to a height of five to ten metres, with a stairway or a ladder that provided access to the top. This was laid out as a platform and surrounded by crenellated walls so as to afford maximum protection to the defence. Heavy cross-bows were hung on the walls, their quivers stiff with arrows, and there were sighting devices with which to direct the shooting accurately. Defensive armour and helmets were provided, and there were supplies of grease and glue for the care and maintenance of weapons. At some sites a pole was erected for hoisting signals, and each tower kept flags, or torches for the purpose. For their daily needs the men stored their water in jars, and they may have been able to convey it in earthenware pipes. There was a brazier stoked with dung on which the section's cooking pot simmered, and some of the posts were equipped with medicine chests. Each post had a supply of builder's tools and materials, and stocks of spare arrows.

The first duty of the sections who manned the watch-towers was to observe enemy movement and take defensive action against any tribesmen who might attempt to rush the Chinese lines or break into their stores. Of equal importance was the task of keeping in regular touch with neighbouring posts, so that no failure of the defences would remain undetected for long, and so that the commandant's headquarters could be kept informed of the situation at the front. Routine signals were exchanged from one post to the next by means of flags or flame, depending on the time of day or night; and for reporting emergencies a section set fire to one of the neat piles of brushwood and timber that always lay stacked behind the lines. All ranks were supposed to be acquainted with the code of signals. A further duty which fell on officers and men was that of inspecting the sandbanks that had been raked smooth on the outer side of the lines and which quickly revealed traces of a human or animal intruder.

Conscripts were also employed on police duties, to prevent the flight of criminals or deserters to areas that lay beyond the grasp of the Han official. Strict controls were kept at recognised points of access to the Chinese lines, and travellers wishing to pass through were asked to show their 'passports'. When the inspecting officer was satisfied with a man's identity, and certain that he was neither on the list of 'persons wanted for arrest', nor carrying contraband goods, his name was entered on the register of transit, with the date and time of his journey and a short description of his means of transport. He was then granted access, inwards or outwards.

In addition the servicemen acted as couriers for the despatch of official mail. There was a system of relay from one post to the next, and a fixed schedule prescribed the time allowed to runners, who sped on their way carrying the rolls of wooden documents. Express deliveries were made on horseback; and specially shaped rods of wood were used for the inscription of emergency orders so that such messages could be conveyed more easily and speedily than the routine reports of military administration.

Some of the men were detached from military duties and assigned to constructional or other work. When they made bricks, which were probably moulded in wooden frames and baked by the sun, they reached an output of 80, or exceptionally 150, a day; they stacked the bricks; and scraped, cleaned, plastered and whitewashed the surfaces of the buildings. As carpenters they kept the wooden equipment in good trim, seeing that the door-bolts could be shot home, or that the pulleys used in raising signals were serviceable. The men were also employed on vegetable gardening or on the collection and storage of fodder for the horses. Some acted as grooms, and some as the cooks who prepared the meals for the nine or ten men of a working party.

Some of the conscripts were put on agricultural work. To solve the problems of supply the government sponsored the utmost use of the land for the production of food locally. The existing water-courses formed the basis of irrigational work, and some of the men were set to digging supplementary channels to bring the water where it could be used most profitably. This project was so important that a special line of fortifications was set up to protect the undertaking; and conscripts who were

26 Considerable pressure was needed to stretch a heavy cross-bow for loading the arrow, which was held in the teeth meanwhile. The two objects on each side of arms are identified variously as quivers or sleeves. A stylised representation

85

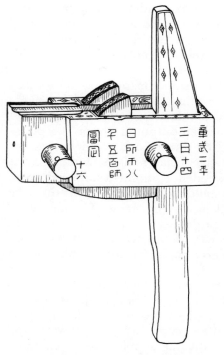

27 A cross-bow trigger; operation of the trigger depressed the claws, which in turn released the arrow. These precision-made mechnisms of bronze were manufactured by the government's agencies, and a note was often inscribed giving the date and place of make and a mark of identification. Exceptionally, this stylised drawing is decorated and the inscription is in a formal style of writing. Dated just after the Han period (A.D. 222)

drafted to work in the official farms may well have found themselves working at tasks to which they were well accustomed in their home villages.

The grain harvested by these men was conveyed to small depots and eventually to one of the large store-houses, of which traces still survive. One of these measured some 185 by 48 metres. Its walls were nearly two metres thick, and a firm base had been laid to protect the grain from the inroads of damp or rodents. Meticulous records were kept both at these and the smaller centres, so that the officials responsible for the stores could account for their receipts and disbursements. For rations were issued to all who were engaged in official business in the area of the static defences; to the conscripts themselves and their families; to officers and their servants; to former convicts, now happily raised from their status on condition that they completed their time in the government's service; or to the men who hailed from the distant commanderies of Shu or Chien-wei (the modern province of Ssu-ch'uan) and were perhaps employed on lumber work in the north-west.

Rations of grain, which was measured in units of volume and not of weight, varied in respect of a man's status, or the age and sex of his immediate relations. In general the daily amount varied between 700 and 2000 cubic centimetres. Some of the men drew rations for their wives and children, or occasionally for a sister or a parent. Records of these transactions may perhaps be taken as evidence that some of the conscripts settled down for long periods at the frontier, and this supposition is supported by lists of the taxable property of a few officers. These included items such as land and houses, vehicles, horses and slaves. It seems improbable that officers would have acquired such possessions for a temporary sojourn of a year or so.

At its best the Han army was organised with a high degree of professionalism, as can be seen from the types of routine reports of which we possess fragments. There were nominal rolls of officers and men, with details of name, age, status and place of origin; there were records of the performances of officers in the course of their duties and of their achievements in the annual tests in archery. There were detailed returns for the employment of servicemen, showing both that they were being profitably employed and that the routine work of the forces was being conducted regularly and continuously. There were signals' logs; registers of the receipt and transit of official documents; financial accounts; lists of stores, which covered such diverse items as weapons of war and officially owned cattle; and there were the inspectors' reports which described faults in the material state of the watch-towers and in the efficiency of their guards. Shorter reports testify to the maintenance of discipline; to attention to the shooting capacity of crossbows; and to the correct procedure for reporting casualties or sickness.

7

The art and practice
of writing

The art and system of writing had been evolved in China some 1500 years before the foundation of the Han dynasty in 202 B.C., but from that time onwards its use became far more general, for political, social and technical reasons alike. For the first time there existed a central government in China which was strong enough to impose uniform procedures over large areas of the sub-continent; and this effect was largely achieved by means of the circulation of the written word. As we have seen, this in turn depended on the emergence of a group of officials, whose education depended largely on the study of early texts, and who frequently enjoyed leisure from their duties which they could devote to the gentle art of letters; and in this way the Han age added substantially to China's literature, often by way of experiment with new forms and styles of prose and poetry.

The new needs of government made it essential to find a standardised form of writing which would serve throughout the provinces, and the style that was brought into fashion in the Han period underwent little change until the end of the imperial age (1911). The commercial and cultural contacts with foreigners who came from India and Central Asia from about 120 B.C. rendered it desirable to reproduce foreign words and names in Chinese texts, and the principles of creating Chinese characters were applied on a far wider scale than hitherto, with extensive and important additions to the Chinese written vocabulary. Finally, Chinese technicians and craftsmen responded to the requirements of the new age by discovering a new medium, of paper, which served alike to communicate the orders of a provincial governor, the learned comments of a scholar or the personal writings of a poet.

Although the actual practice of writing was confined to a few select members of society, who can almost be regarded as forming professional groups, the formative effect of these activities has been of paramount importance. It has led to the steady dissemination of cultural influences of a uniform nature, and sometimes to the elimination of local practices that had arisen among a wild and unlettered people.

The Chinese system of writing is not based on the use of a limited number of signs which express the phonetic elements of a word; it embraces a large number of symbols or characters, each one of which denotes an object or abstract concept. The development of the characters was affected by two evolutionary processes, which can be traced from about 1500 B.C. to their culmination in the Han period, but which are by no means yet complete. The first can be described as the growth of intellectual maturity. This was seen in the need to express more ideas or abstractions in writing, and resulted in the formation of a large number of new characters to supplement the 3000 or so already in use by 202 B.C. Indeed, as a result of the activities of the writers and scholars of the Han period over 9000 characters were included in China's first dictionary, presented to the throne in A.D. 121; although not all were in general use.

The second process was a technical one that concerned the medium on which the written text was conveyed. For the first thousand years of writing, the Chinese usually engraved their characters in hard substances—at first shell or bone, and, later, bronze; but from about 300 B.C. or perhaps earlier a radical change set in, as a result of which writing was henceforth effected by painting or inscribing the characters on silk or wood, and eventually paper. This change both followed the growing need for simplification and stimulated the more general use of writing and a quicker means of education.

To understand these processes more fully it is necessary to revert in time to the pre-imperial age. China's first written records appear in the form of inscriptions that were engraved on bones or shells that had been used in a procedure for fore-telling the future. Before embarking on a major venture, such as a military campaign or a hunting expedition, the kings of the

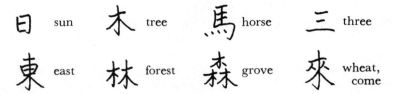

28 The modern forms of Chinese characters are essentially identical
with those of the Han period

Shang kingdom (*c.* 1500–1000 B.C.) were in the habit of asking
advice from unseen supernatural powers. An intermediary
priest prepared a piece of tortoise-shell or a bone of a sacrificial
animal, by drilling a hole at a suitable place; and from the
cracks that appeared when the shells or bones were heated he
was able to infer whether the outcome of the scheme would be
successful or not. The priests then wrote down the questions,
the answers that had been reached, and, occasionally, a short
account of what had actually occurred.

Some of the symbols which they used were pictograms (e.g.,
a simple drawing of objects such as 'sun', 'horse', 'tree'); others
conveyed an idea or abstract (e.g., three horizontal straight
lines symbolised 'three'). But in time the priests needed to
express more complex ideas, or to symbolise words which
formed part of everyday speech but which could not be shown
by drawing a picture or abstract symbol. In a few cases the
elements of the language were such that it was possible to adapt
an existing character that had been used for another purpose,
e.g., to render the word known today as *lai*, and meaning 'to
come', it was possible to write a symbol used to express another
word *lai*, meaning 'wheat'; and once the convention was known,
a reader would be able to discriminate from the context.

There were other devices which were invented by China's
scribes well before the Han period. A single character was
sometimes formed by placing two or more pictograms together,
in close proximity, so that several ideas could be expressed in an
intimate association and the reader could draw the obvious
inference. Thus two or three trees together signified a forest;
or a view of the sun behind a tree could be used to indicate
the quarter where the sun rises, i.e. the east.

From early days (perhaps 1000 B.C.) scribes were finding ways of combining characters that already existed to convey more exact meanings. For it had come about quite naturally that a character such as *sheng* (i), meaning 'birth', had been used to express certain meanings by extension, e.g. (*a*) born of woman, or clan-name; or (*b*) innate feelings. To emphasise that the character was being used in one of these more specialised senses, the scribes took to adding a second element by the side, e.g., for (*a*) that of a woman (iv) and for (*b*) that of a heart (v); and the newly evolved characters (ii) and (iii) would not be open to ambiguous interpretation.

There was a further way in which two elements could be combined to form a single new unit, that was practised extensively during the Han period. Here the intention was deliberately to evolve a means of conveying a word that was in general use and which sounded like others whose meaning was utterly different. So one existing character, which was well-known and whose pronunciation could not be in any doubt, was combined with another character whose meaning was clear to the reader; and he would be able to discriminate between symbols such as (vi) 'late', (vii) 'to summon', and (viii) 'a grave' (pronounced anciently as *mag* and today as *mu*); or (xi) 'star', (xii) 'monkey', and (xiii) 'to awake from a drunken stupor' (pronounced *sieng* anciently, and *hsing* today). In these characters, (ix) conveys 'strength', (x) 'earth', (xiv) 'dog', and (xv) 'wine-vessel'.

Many of the characters that had been evolved from the

29 Again, these modern characters are essentially the same as those of Han times

earliest days before the Han empire are still in general use, and, despite the changes that have occurred in the materials used for writing, their shapes are still recognisably the same. Highly complex styles were in fashion for the inscriptions that were made on the sacred bronze vessels in the pre-imperial age (i.e. from about 1500 to 250 B.C.). For these objects bore not only a legal and religious value; they also formed a magnificent medium of expression for China's early artists, and the highly decorated patterns and designs called for a somewhat more detailed attention to the written characters of the inscriptions than had been suitable for the early incisions made for oracular purposes. From about 1000 B.C. onwards there was a tendency for greater beautification and complication of the written characters. But the process of forming larger political units, which culminated in the imperial unification of 221 B.C. both depended on and stimulated simplification and standardisation, with the result that the script of the Han officials and scholars has remained the norm until the present time.

As we have seen, most of the earliest inscriptions were made as engravings scratched on bone or shell, but in some cases the priests painted their signs with a brush. From perhaps about 300 B.C. the brush came to take first place as the usual tool of the scribe, and it is only very recently that it has yielded to the fountain pen or ball-point stylus. The brush was used in the first instance on silk and wood, and it is only natural that very few specimens survive of the texts that were written on those highly perishable substances. The single extant piece of inscribed silk that dates from before the imperial age was found recently in central China; and both the content of the document and its coloured designs are connected more with magic and mysticism than with the life of the educated members of society. But we do know of the use of the brush and silken roll in high quarters during the Han dynasty. In those days the art of writing was still confined to a very small element of the population, and silk was an expensive and much-prized commodity. Some of the texts that were prepared directly for use inside the palace were probably written as de luxe copies on silk. Such rolls could be handled conveniently, and the tapes needed to fasten the roll could doubtless be prepared in a form suitable for the emperor's own fingers to unloosen. Some literary

30 Roll of wooden strips: each strip carries one column of writing. Long strips (2·2 Han feet, or 50 cm.) were used for some of the classical texts, as here, and shorter strips (1 foot, 23 cm.) for less important works and copies of administrative documents. This reconstruction shows the roll fully closed, so that the text is invisible. The title and number of the chapter can be seen on the reverse side of the strips.

works were written on silk, as were the maps or diagrams that formed part of the administrative records, or textbooks on subjects such as astrology, divination or medicine.

But the main work of the Han scribe who turned out copies of the government's orders or listed the items of stores that were in his charge was done on wood. Such documents were heavy and cumbersome, as compared with the delicate rolls used in the court; but wood was cheap and in plentiful supply; and although it may have been more fragile in the course of transit, a wooden document could be stored with less danger of immediate decay. Surviving finds are more plentiful than those of silk, and include parts of documents that were written mostly between 100 B.C. and A.D. 300. Most of the pieces are of wood but there are some of bamboo; the greater part come from administrative documents but there are a few precious examples of literary texts.

Before use, the sap was dried out of the wood, which was then cut to standard sizes. Single boards were shaped and planed for texts whose length was limited and predictable; and some pieces were specially prepared as triangular prisms, or long rods for particular purposes. But for longer texts, or those whose compilation was not completed at a single session, general practice was to use a succession of narrow strips. There were several standard sizes during the Han period, depending partly on the type of text that was being written. The longest strips of all, which measured 2·4 or 3 feet* were used for copies of the Statutes, Ordinances and Imperial Edicts that were

---

* i.e. the Han foot which measured approximately 23 cm or 9¼ inches; for weights and measures see p. 196.

31 A scribe's equipment: the tip of this writing brush, from the north-west of the empire, is almost worn away. The knife was used to clean text off strips for re-use. An inscription on the back shows this one to date from A.D. 184

circulated among offices; and some of the more important literary texts used in schooling were written on long strips of 2·2 or 2·4 feet, which carried 60 or 100, or exceptionally 120 characters each. The less important literary texts which featured in the schoolroom were written on shorter strips (1·2 or 0·8 feet); but the regular strips used for the records, reports and registers of the civil service measured one foot.

The strips were narrow and thin, and it was usual to write on one side only. Hempen strings were passed alternately above and below consecutive strips, and special grooves were sometimes cut to retain them in their correct positions. The whole document could then be fastened in the form of a roll, for purposes of transport or storage. An alternative type of writing tablet was provided by somewhat thicker strips, with a hole drilled neatly at the head. Such pieces could be inscribed on two or more sides, with the text running from one to the next. The fastening was contrived by means of a single string which was threaded through the holes at the top of the pieces, so that each one could be turned in the reader's hands, and all the surfaces examined.

Usually the surfaces prepared for writing were narrow, being designed to accommodate a single column of characters only. If consecutive columns appeared on the same strip they were read from right to left, and the strips were taken in that order. Of the scribe's equipment, the brush was made by binding three shafts together and surmounting these with a head of deer's hair or, at a later date, rabbit's fur. For erasing errors the scribe used a knife, and this also served for peeling the

94

wooden strips clean so that they could be re-used for a second or third time. Accidental omissions could sometimes be rectified if the text had been laid out with sufficiently deep spaces between the characters, and in some texts dots were inserted for punctuation. Usually a margin was left at the top and foot of each column, and this practice enabled a scribe to put in a heading, boldly separated from the rest of the text. In one example, serial numbers appear at the foot of strips which formed parts of a copy of a literary text.

When a document was complete its strips could be rolled together for convenience, as can be seen in fig. 30. For despatch, the strings which bound the strips could be secured by means of clay, which set hard over the strings; and it was the regular practice for officials to impress their seals of office in the clay before it had hardened. This impression could then be used to identify the originator of a document without breaking the seal or unrolling the strips; and at the same time the seal acted as a mark of authentication.

Seals were one of the means of distinguishing rank and status. Three different words were used in Han China with the meaning of seal, and usage depended on the person concerned. Thus, the emperor's 'signet' was not to be confused with a senior official's 'stamp' or a junior clerk's 'chop'. Of the many examples of Han seals that have been found, some are inscribed with the title of an office, some with an official's name and some with both. There are also surviving squares of clay which had been baked hard, and where the impression is still intact. Seals could also be used with ink on silk.

Silk rolls, then, lined the shelves of the emperor's personal collection of books, and may have been owned by some of the wealthier of Han scholars. And the office-files consisted of the more bulky and durable rolls of wooden strips, neatly bundled together, with a tag hanging down from each one to declare its contents. Meanwhile the Han period saw the evolution of a new substance, which would soon come into general use for book-production and would be in service two thousand years later. In all probability, paper was not introduced suddenly. In the prevailing scarcity and high cost of silk, somebody perhaps thought of experimenting with the waste fibres of silk, and the first production of a paper-like substance may have occurred

32 Seals were used by officials as emblems of authority and for authenticating documents. The top was often shaped as a loop, or an animal such as a tortoise or serpent, and allowed for the attachment of a fastening cord. The characters were incised on the base, in reverse, and after pressure on an ink or wax pad, the seal's impression showed white characters against a black or scarlet background

during the process. Traditionally, the Chinese date the invention of paper in A.D. 105, when a named official is said to have conveyed the idea to the throne. Ts'ai Lun was at this time responsible for those agencies which manufactured the equipment needed in the palace, and he is reported to have compounded his paper from materials such as the bark of trees, hemp, old rags and fish-nets. It is quite impossible to judge how quickly the new substance went into circulation; and although there may be a few scraps of paper which can possibly be dated in the Han period, the first authentic pieces are dated in A.D. 310 and 312. It can probably be assumed that paper was coming into regular use during the third and fourth centuries, but that the use of silk and wood was not yet completely outmoded.

While paper, a highly perishable substance, was gaining currency, scholars of Han China were also preparing written monuments of a far more lasting nature. To establish an authorised version of the works associated with Confucius and his teachings whose accuracy would be beyond question, it was decided that a standard text should be engraved on stone tablets which would be solemnly and safely preserved for posterity. The project was started in A.D. 175, and it took eight years to complete the task. Altogether some forty to fifty stones were needed to provide adequate surfaces for engraving the 200,000 characters of the selected texts. If we are to believe the histories, crowds of scholars visited the capital city to see the stones; and it may have been possible for them to make *facsimile* copies of the inscriptions on the newfangled material that Ts'ai Lun had introduced, so that a learned man could retire to his own home to study his own copy of the standard text of the scriptures.

This incident set a precedent which was to be followed by later dynasties in China and had some effect on the official promotion of printing in the tenth century. But stone tablets also featured in a different context in Han society, in the memorial monuments which were set up for the dead. These were made for prominent officials whose careers were terminated honourably by death or retirement rather than by disgrace or dismissal for a shameful cause. The epitaphs record the ancestry of the deceased, together with a list of the offices which he had filled and the successful exploits for which he had been judged responsible. The language of the monuments is conventional and may appear to be somewhat fulsome; and a reader may perhaps wonder how such paragons of behaviour could ever live in mere mortal guise. But the testimony of the inscriptions is by no means valueless. It tells how minor officials or the followers of a great man would club together to erect a memorial for their patron; it tells of the pride that the Han official had in his ancestry and of his desire for permanent recognition of his services.

Finally there were occasions when it was desirable to possess a permanent record of a contract. If a man bought a plot of land to build a tomb, the text of the deed of sale was sometimes written on the walls by brush; and post-Han practices permit the supposition that copies of such agreements were sometimes made on lengths of lead or pewter, which were intended for burial at a suitable location and for subsequent quotation should the title of ownership be brought into question.

8

Literature and the
intellect

In 26 B.C. the Han emperor ordered copies of literary works to be assembled at the capital from all commanderies and kingdoms. There were two reasons for this measure: first, to ensure that the imperial collection would be as complete as possible; and, secondly, to enable different versions of a text to be compared and a 'correct' edition preserved in the imperial library. The scholars who were engaged on this task prepared a list of the copies which they had examined, and this list of titles happily survives to constitute the earliest catalogue that we possess of the contents of a Chinese library. The silken scrolls, supplemented by the more normal wooden rolls, which lay stacked on the emperor's shelves included a large variety of writings.

First there were the texts of the sacred classical works associated with the saintly kings of China's distant and mythological past, and partly ascribed to the editorship of Confucius. We have met these works already, in connection with both the schooling of officials and the project for engraving stone tablets of an authorised version in A.D. 175. The imperial library contained copies of different recensions of these texts, together with different traditional ancillary works and the commentaries of several academic schools. There were copies of the sayings of the many philosophers who had argued or preached in China before and after the formation of the empire, and there was a variety of works of a technical nature, classified by subjects such as divination, mathematics, medicine, warfare, agriculture or astronomy.

History writing was well advanced by the time that the

catalogue was being compiled. The first of China's standard histories, which was completed in about 90 B.C. and still survives, was a work of 130 chapters, which took as their subject the history of man in this world from the earliest times until the contemporary period of the author. This work formed a model that has been followed by official historians throughout the imperial age.

Many of the books whose titles appear in the catalogue have long since been lost, but the tantalising evidence of quotations that appear in later works and of the titles themselves makes it possible to appreciate the degree of intellectual sophistication that had been reached by this time. Already there were the beginnings of literary criticism, in the form of attempts to interpret the texts of the pre-imperial age which were now some five centuries or more old, written in verbiage that was obsolete and partly incomprehensible. The philosophers had never tired of stressing the worth of moral values, particularly in connection with the practical work of organising a state or forming a just and contented society. They had appreciated that the human race had evolved from a state of savagery, and recognised the need to replace old superstitious practices, sometimes marked by brutality or violence, by rules of conduct that were designed to discipline and educate the human character. Statesmen were writing tracts on political theory and practice, arguing perhaps on matters of principle, perhaps on specific measures of government. And some Chinese writers had tried to penetrate the mysteries of those unseen forces which apparently controlled many of man's ventures in the world.

Many of the early creations of Chinese literature, that date long before the Han period, had been written to instruct rather than to please, to teach rather than to satisfy emotional urges; and a high proportion of Han writings originated from just such motives. But the catalogue of works in the imperial library furnishes considerable evidence of the new literary forms and styles that were now being moulded. The Han age produced poetry designed to afford lyrical delight, and depending no longer on a musical accompaniment, as had China's earliest poems. Court writers were composing long descriptive pieces, sometimes so as to flatter the throne and its achievements, sometimes so as to describe the luxurious life of the palace.

A collection of short poems of the age reveals an appreciation of natural beauty and a depth of human emotions, as can be seen in the following examples, for whose English version we are indebted to the late Arthur Waley:

Green, green,
The grass by the river bank.
Thick, thick,
The willow trees in the garden.
Sad, sad,
The lady in the tower.
White, white,
Sitting at the casement window.

Fair, fair,
Her red-powdered face.
Small, small,
She puts out her pale hand.
Once she was a dancing-house girl,
Now she is a wandering man's wife.
The wandering man went, but did not return.
It is hard alone to keep an empty bed.

or

The bright moon, oh how white it shines,
Shines down on the gauze curtains of my bed!
Racked by sorrow I toss and cannot sleep;
Picking up my clothes, I wander up and down.
My absent love says that he is happy,
But I would rather he said he was coming back.
Out in the courtyard I stand hesitating, alone;
To whom can I tell the sad thoughts I think?
Staring before me I enter my room again;
Falling tears wet my mantle and robe.

The next chapter will show something of the prevalence in Han times of an irrational outlook that coloured many aspects of both public and private life. A belief in various types of occult powers together with attempts to manipulate them, so that they would be favourably inclined to the fortunes of the living, featured conspicuously in the theory and practice of Han government. For from about 100 B.C., the palace had adopted certain philosophical doctrines which succeeded in both satisfying these cravings and presenting the moralist views and disciplinary precepts of the school of Confucius. The association of these two widely diverging attitudes was no mere foible of the intellect; nor was it an emotional reaction of a few isolated individuals; it affected deeply the conduct of major activities of state. The unseen powers were believed to exercise a control on the emperor's fortunes; they were invoked as a means of compelling loyal obedience from a gullible public; past history was interpreted in the light of their influence; and the measures of the present were sometimes shaped so as to conform with a forecast of those powers' activities in the future.

Some of the steps taken to placate these forces were seemingly harmless, for example, the selection of a specially favoured colour for the dynasty, or the avowal that one of the material elements (such as fire or water) was at that juncture exercising a dominating influence in the cosmic order. But similar measures could be highly dangerous and insidious if they led to political action that was otherwise unjustified, or if they closed the minds of leading statesmen or emperors to the demands of a rational explanation of the world and its phenomena.

Several protestant voices made themselves heard at this time, to decry the excesses of their contemporaries, and to reaffirm the view that the course of natural and human history must be explained in terms of reason. Wang Ch'ung (A.D. 27–c. 100) is perhaps the most famous critic of the times owing to the survival of the greater part of his essays, which consisted originally of 85 chapters. This was an age when nature's mighty forces were felt only too violently but understood only too rarely. Wang Ch'ung insisted that the uncontrollable catastrophes of storm, earthquake, drought or landslide were not brought about by the desire of a heavenly force to warn an emperor of his imperfections, so that he would mend his ways and save his people from destruction. Wang Ch'ung affirmed that disasters sprang from natural causes, from imbalances of temperature or climate, and that they formed but a usual part in nature's rhythmic processes of growth, change and decay. Certainly, according to Wang Ch'ung, no explanation should be sought in the exercise of moral considerations by natural forces; nor was man's enjoyment of health, wealth or prosperity to be correlated with his moral qualities or conduct. According to Wang Ch'ung, man is certainly the servant of destiny; but destiny is no power to be manipulated by symbolic practices or magic. Man's failings and lack of independence are only too obvious, and misguided notions such as the belief in ghosts were engendered by man's physical weakness and his hallucinations.

Wang Ch'ung's attitude can be described as scientific, in so far as he believed that the world is to be explained on rational principles, without recourse to the miraculous, and that their truth can be demonstrated by the collection and verification of data. There were other manifestations in the Han age of a systematic intellect and its application to material problems. Mathematicians had addressed themselves to problems such as that of calculating the relationship between the diameter and circumference of a circle, or of extracting the square and cube roots of numbers. As an aid to counting they may have used rods, but the idea of an abacus was probably not evolved much before the sixth century. Systems of measuring length, area, volume and weight were based sometimes on a decimal metric scale, sometimes on a less regular progression of units (see p. 196). For the practical application of mathematics, there were rules and formulae for calculating the area or capacity of a wide variety of figures such as a square, rhomboid, or circle, cube, pyramid or prism.

Some of the tasks of the Han servicemen, such as the ex-

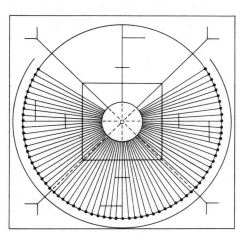

33 On sun-dials besides the central socket, each line of graduations ended with a small hole, and the serial numbers 1–69 (not shown here), were inscribed against each one, in a clock-wise direction. The horizontal markings within and without the circle were probably used to note or measure some astronomical feature

change of routine signals, or the maintenance of schedules for communications, depended on accurate time-keeping, and mathematics figured conspicuously in the means of defining and measuring such periods. Poles were used to measure the length of the sun's shadow, and from those observations the occurrence of the solstices could be awaited with some confidence. A sun-dial that was used in the first or second century B.C. was designed on the principle of dividing the entire period of the day and night into 100 sections. Sixty-nine graduations, numbered consecutively in a clockwise direction, are marked on an area of just over two thirds of the face of the dial; and these provided sufficient space to show the fall of the sun's shadow even on the longest day of the year. With such an instrument the passage of time could be followed with considerable accuracy.

The hundred sections of the day and night were related to the major division of this period of time into 12 hours (i.e. each hour was equivalent to two hours of modern time), and these were denoted by various systems. The regular designations in use by the Han servicemen were formed by descriptive terms, such as 'cock-crow', 'dawn' etc., so that moments in time were defined in terms such as 'dinner hour and three sections', or 'sunset, 4'. In addition to sun-dials, water-clocks were in use by 100 B.C.; but these can only have been rudimentary devices as compared with the highly complicated mechanisms of the eleventh century, which were scrupulously designed by engineers and craftsmen, both to tell the time of day and to declare the positions of the heavenly bodies in the firmament.

The regulation of the calendar and its promulgation featured as one of the responsibilities of imperial government from early days. For the calendar was of the utmost importance in the arrangement of agricultural work and in certain seasonal tasks of administration, such as the collection of tax. Moreover, it was intimately bound up with the will of many Chinese to avoid thwarting the harmony of the natural world or the forces of the occult powers. To fix the calendar correctly, it was necessary to observe the stars accurately; and such observation depended on the use of precise instruments and an accurate means of calculation.

The Chinese calendar was arranged to take account of the cycles of the earth and the moon. The moon's movements, repeating every 29 and a fraction days, could be observed fairly easily and accurately; but to regulate seasonal work, it was necessary to reconcile this cycle with the earth's period of 365 and a fraction days. The calendar was made up of long months (of 30 days) and short months (of 29 days) which usually alternated with each other. Normally there were 12 months in the year, but as a means of keeping the calendar in step with the motions of the earth and the moon, an extra or intercalary month had to be inserted every 32 or 33 months, with the result that every third year or so the calendar for the year extended for 13 months. In regulating the calendar it was necessary to lay down which months in the year would be long and which would be short, and to decide the point at which the extra, or leap, month was to be inserted.

At first, years were enumerated in series from the beginning of an emperor's reign, but from 134 B.C. onwards it became customary to introduce a new reign-title, or expression by which dates were to be known, at other times as well. This was done every five or six years, and the practice could be used as a means of advertising the good fortune that attended the government, the success of its policies, or its aims. Thus, a new emperor, who was later known as Ch'eng ti, acceded in 33 B.C., and from the following year the era was entitled *Chien-shih* (a phrase which corresponds to a modern catch-word such as 'The New Establishment'). The years were now designated *Chien-shih* 1 (i.e. 32 B.C.), *Chien-shih* 2 (31 B.C.) etc. But a change came in 28 B.C., when the government proudly announced that it had brought the Yellow River under control, and that the achievement would be marked by choosing a new reign-title, and designating the current year as the first year of *Ho-p'ing*, or 'Pacification of the River'.

The system of denoting days of the month by a serial number running from 1 to 29 or 30 probably became current during the first century A.D. Before then the practice was to designate each day by one of a series of 60 written expressions, formed by two characters each. The complete series of 60 terms thus extended over one complete month and portions of two other months before it was necessary to revert to the beginning of the series (it was just possible for the series to cover two complete months, one long and one short, preceded or followed by the last or first day of a third month). Copies of the calendar, which were prepared by government officials on wooden strips, consisted of a list of the terms by which consecutive days were designated. These were set out so as to show at a glance the length of the months and the position, if any, of an intercalary month. There was also room to include seasonal information such as the occurrence of the solstices.

There were other spheres of human activity in which the Chinese intellect was making strides during the Han period. Physicians were diagnosing and treating diseases, keeping case books and lists of prescriptions. One medical treatise describes the symptoms of a disease which might be known today as diabetes, and which is termed in the text 'fever of the spleen':

> This disease is due to the consumption of large quantities of sweet and fat substances. Fats induce internal fever and sweets bring about a feeling of satiety, with a resultant rise of the vital breath and feelings of thirst.

Fragments of prescriptions which have been found at sites occupied by Han servicemen in the north-west include remedies for ailments of both men and horses. One of these reads as follows:

For feverish colds, four ingredients:

Wu hui [*Aconitum uncinatum*, L.]	10 parts
Chü [*Atractylis ovata*, Th.]	10 parts
Hsi hsin [*Aristolachia Sieboldi*, Miq.]	6 parts
Kuei [*Camphora Loueiri*, Nees. (M)]	4 parts

One dose to be taken in hot water three times daily and twice nightly; will bring relief by bowel movement and urination, without causing perspiration.

One of the most brilliant, but by no means typical, examples of intellectual achievement of the Han age is seen in the work of Chang Heng (A.D. 78–139) who came from Nan-yang (the modern province of Hu-pei). He was a member of a prominent family, and his grandfather had served as a governor of a commandery. As a boy Chang Heng is said to have applied himself to bookwork, and was sent to attend classes in the capital city. Here he gained the requisite familiarity with the scriptural texts of the classics, and was apparently all set to embark on an official career. However, he seems to have been reluctant to do so, and set himself to compose a descriptive piece of poetical writing, on the glories of the two capital cities of the Han dynasty. In time, Chang Heng was actually appointed to an official post, but his main interests lay in science and technology. He applied himself to the problems of mathematics, astronomy and geography, designing a number of instruments to aid his researches. He calculated the value of π to be 3·1622, the most accurate approximation that had yet been made in China. In interpreting the motions of the heavenly bodies and their relation to the earth, he followed theories that had long been known, but thanks to his logical application, his conclusions reached a new depth of understanding and a new standard of precision. He observed carefully the move-

34 Reconstruction of a bronze seismograph made by Chang Heng in A.D. 132. When a shock occurred the pendulum would swing along a track and dislodge one of eight horizontal arms from its resting place, thus opening the jaws of one of eight dragons. From a warning sound and the fall of a ball from the mouth of the dragon into that of the toad below, an observer knew that a shock had occurred and the direction of the affected area

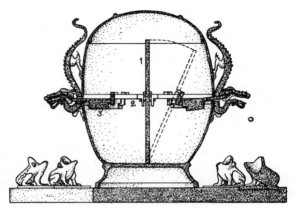

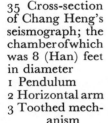

35 Cross-section of Chang Heng's seismograph; the chamber of which was 8 (Han) feet in diameter
1 Pendulum
2 Horizontal arm
3 Toothed mechanism

ments of the stars and marked their positions on charts. About A.D. 125 he made important improvements to devices which had been designed to measure distances and define points in the heavens; and an armillary sphere which he had constructed was rotated by regulated water-power. It is likely that Chang Heng evolved the use of a grid-system for the purpose of cartography; and he is perhaps best known to the western world for his production of a seismograph. This instrument comprised a central column, delicately poised so that an earth tremor displaced a needle from its otherwise constant position, and released one of eight balls to indicate the direction from which the quake had made itself felt.

Instruments of this type can hardly be said to have featured in the everyday life of the Chinese of the Han period, any more than for any generation of men. Their production at this juncture was due partly to official motivation, partly to the spirit of intellectual enquiry of a few individuals and partly to Chang Heng's own personal contribution. But whatever their general application to daily life, the instruments demonstrate the degree to which scientific and technological skills had advanced by the second century A.D., and they form the essential forerunners of the more complicated and refined devices of a later age.

9

Religion and the
occult powers

Many elements can be distinguished in the religious and superstitious beliefs and practices of Han China. There was a deep-seated belief in prognosticating the future; men tried to serve the spirits of their departed ancestors, to placate beings which were thought to be malevolent and to accord due reverence to personified powers of nature. There was a faith in the protecting powers extended by Heaven to the emperor and his dispensation; but at times of political intrigue, attempts were made to interfere with the imperial succession by means of imprecation. A yearning for immortality expressed itself in a number of forms. Some theorists had explained the creation of the universe and the operation of its natural cycles as the result of two overwhelming forces and their interaction with the material elements of which the world was composed; and a faith in these doctrines persuaded some of the need to regulate their behaviour and to adopt symbolic patterns so as to comply with these inescapable rhythms. In some areas, particularly in the south, there survived local practices of a dubious nature, which involved a trust in intermediaries and the contacts they made with occult powers through trance or ecstasy. By contrast the followers of Confucius' precepts sought to give a lead to human behaviour in the light of moral principles and to detract from a faith in irrational powers as a guide to life.

It was clearly in the interests of the emperor and the government to foster a popular belief in the favours that a supernatural Heaven extended to the ruling house, and there were some occasions when political leaders tried deliberately to exploit a faith in omens so as to captivate support. Towards the end of the

Han period there began a process which led to the association of these cravings and instincts with some of China's early mystical writings, and to the establishment of religious communities who followed prescribed procedures or rites with which to benefit body or soul; and from the first century A.D. there arrived on the Chinese scene the first propagators of the Buddhist faith, which was destined to play so large a part in China's intellectual, cultural and social development.

One of the nine major departments of the Han government was concerned with matters of religion, and its complement included special officials who were responsible for prayer, the upkeep of shrines or similar duties. The attention of the state to these matters was no innovation of the Han house, but came as an heritage from the pre-imperial kingdoms; for these had been no less anxious to secure earthly blessings from unseen powers. But under a single imperial dispensation religious practices could be observed in a more regular manner and with a wider application. There was every reason for the government to formalise the practices and to formulate current concepts. This could be done in a manner suited to the idea of an empire resting on a single, central government, presided over by an emperor who was acting on Heaven's behalf and who was responsible to Heaven for the physical and moral well-being of the inhabitants of earth. The government therefore took a hand in prescribing the rites that were to be performed in honour of the spirits, or to appease those powers thought capable of making or marring human happiness. The state provided for shrines to be built to honour the lords of the rain or the winds, or the guardian spirits of certain holy rivers or mountains. Each locality in the empire was commanded to conduct its own worship and sacrifices to the local protecting spirits and to maintain the intermediaries by whose agency man could make contact with the occult. These spirits included the lords of the soil and of the crops, who were entitled to receive seasonal reverence and offerings of sheep or swine.

From the beginning of Chinese civilisation, members of the same clan had acknowledged and worshipped the authority of their deceased ancestors; for, dead though they were, their powers were thought to be no less overawing than those of the contemporary leader who was their descendant. The cult of the

Han emperor's ancestors became an expensive undertaking, as shrines were erected in many of the provinces as well as the capital city. Each shrine was served with its offering of food and its sacrifices of sheep or pigs; the maintenance of priests with their attendant acolytes and musicians added to the expense, as did the sentinels who kept guard over these holy places; and from time to time protests were raised against this use of funds and suggestions made to reduce the number of the shrines.

Further expenditure was involved in the visits paid by the emperor to holy sites for the purpose of performing special ceremonies. Very often the districts through which he passed were obliged to provide the necessities of life for his entourage, and it was necessary to offset this burden by exempting such areas from taxation. The most important religious undertaking of this type was the pilgrimage to Mount T'ai, in east China. This was intended to invoke the blessing of Heaven on the ruler and to confirm the authority of which he stood possessed. At the same time the conspicuous way in which the mission was accomplished served to advertise its ideals to his subjects.

The successful ascent of Mount T'ai by a Chinese emperor took place very rarely throughout imperial history. The first Ch'in emperor managed the feat in 219 B.C., but, despite later statements, in all probability he did not perform elaborate ceremonies of the type that were conducted later. The Han emperor Wu ti made the ascent on several occasions from 110 B.C., but little can be said regarding the rites as these were carried out with the utmost secrecy. Luckily there is more information for the visit paid by Kuang Wu ti in A.D. 56, and it is likely that the ceremonies performed then were repeated on the very few subsequent occasions when an emperor climbed the mountain for ritual purposes (666, 725 and 1008; in addition the same type of ceremony was performed at a different mountain in 695).

Mount T'ai was one of nature's conspicuously mighty creations. It was regarded as an object of veneration which could answer prayers for blessings; and it also seems that the mountain or its spirit was looked upon as an intermediary with whom prayers could be deposited for transmission to the real powers of the cosmos, those of Heaven and Earth. When an emperor made the ascent he sacrificed four times, twice to Heaven

36 Bronze mirror: reverse side, showing mythical figures such as the Queen Mother of the West (see p. 114). Late second century A.D.

37 Tile-end (see p. 133 and figure 50) showing the Red Bird symbol of the South (see p. 118)

and twice to Earth. He went there to report on his successful tenure of his office and to pray for its continuation. The whole rite symbolised the mystical union between those powers and the emperor, who sacrificed bulls and raised ritual mounds as part of the service. Above all, he deposited documents in the form of inscribed jade tablets, which were securely held in special caskets of stone. These documents probably gave an account of his stewardship in the past and included prayers for the future. Other aspirations, such as the attainment of perpetual living, the search for the company of immortal beings and the artificial production of gold later became involved with the properties possessed by Mount T'ai.

The spirit of the soil was worshipped at various levels of the state hierarchy, as it concerned the emperor, the officials and the people. A mound or altar marked the sacred spot where the spirit was thought to be accessible, and his intervention was sought by sacrifices and drum-beating, to bring about a state of fertility. The spirit was also associated with evil acts of nature such as eclipses or excessive rains; and at such times there was performed a ceremony of restraining him, by tying a red cord around the spot associated with his presence. At times of drought steps were taken to encourage his active intervention for good, by purifying the altar.

In addition, members of the imperial house and senior officials believed in other sorts of occult power. These beliefs sometimes led to actions which affected the daily lives of the population, and it is likely that non-literate members of society harboured the same faith. On one occasion, in about 30 B.C., there were signs that the Yellow River would soon be causing one of its periodic inundations. The provincial governor led his subordinate officials in person to the river bank and took steps to appease the river's mighty ruling spirit. He had a grey horse cast as an offering into the waters; and, holding jade emblems that were thought to possess magical authority, he had the intermediary shamans recite their imprecations. The level of the water still rose, and all the local inhabitants fled, leaving the governor to stand alone with one assistant. Eventually the waters abated, and in due course an edict was proclaimed praising the governor for his steadfast valour and granting him promotion and a bounty of gold.

The cult of immortality, which was of paramount importance in the growth of religious practices in Han China, derived from early origins. A desire to prolong life is seen in some of the first records of thought and emotion that date from the eighth century B.C. or even earlier. It was probably inspired not only as a matter of personal interest for the individual but also as a means of ensuring the continuity or survival of the man's family or community, and it is possible to discern two distinct ways in which the concept was being advanced in the fourth and third centuries B.C.

In the first place there was a longing for physical immortality, for the continuation of life in the world of the flesh without suffering the failures, corruption and destruction of the body; such an idea of immortality was essentially this-worldly. But at the same time there was developing a belief that it was possible to attain the bliss of an endless life in the totally different circumstances of another world; and the characteristics of those who attained a non-worldly immortality of this type were those of the ascetic or the hermit.

Both these objectives could be reached by the intervention of intermediary experts. These were the magicians who could lay their hands on the medicaments and drugs that would preserve the body; alternatively they could devise means of introduction to those who had already achieved a state of non-worldly immortality, and who could possibly lead others to the enjoyment of the same life of enchantment. On several occasions in the late third and the second centuries B.C. emperors sent expeditions to search for non-worldly immortals, whose abode was thought to lie beyond the confines of the known world; and in this way we hear of parties who explored the Eastern Isles of the Ocean, to find immortal beings, and of the thought that the Queen Mother of the West who could confer these blessings would be found in the deep recesses of Central Asia.

Despite their apparent inconsistency there was a tendency for these two concepts of a deathless existence to become associated together, partly on account of the devices and ideas of the intermediaries. There were emperors who busied themselves with ceremonies and pilgrimages that were designed to achieve one or the other state; and it was sometimes possible to

38 Tomb fresco showing service to spiritual powers; a dead man, accompanied by a page, meets a spirit who will guide him in his future life among the birds and beings shown on the left. The three figures below are worshipping the spirits of the dead with their offerings on a table and three cups below. Four more tables lie to the right

combine an attempt to achieve immortality with the prayers directed to Heaven for its blessing of imperial rule. However, the cult of immortality was by no means restricted to members of the imperial family or the court. The idea of a non-worldly immortality became popularised and was transformed some-what drastically in the process. It no longer implied the simple transfer of an individual to live endlessly in a sphere that lay beyond the confines of the known world; the idea came to imply the wholesale removal there of a man's family, household and creature comforts. A retinue would thus accompany its master to his new life; and as well as partaking of its joys they would be able to serve him in their accustomed way, and main-tain his household in a correct and suitable style. These results could be achieved if all members of the household were willing to receive the necessary drugs; and in one well-known instance a man smeared his very house with these precious liquids to bring about the transformation.

Drugs then were used not only as a means of preserving the body and ensuring a state of deathlessness in this world, but also to achieve a removal to a non-worldly state of immortality. A belief in bodily deathlessness persisted in popular circles and amongst the more educated members of society, as the sceptical protests of a few rationalist thinkers remind us. But these lone voices did little to dispel the urge to prolong a physical existence or to eliminate the use of potions that were designed to defeat death. There were those who imbibed liquids compounded of pearls and gold; or who tried to lighten the body's weight; or who regulated their breathing to achieve such ends. There is also some evidence of a belief that the successful removal to another existence depended on the quality of a man's conduct in this world and on Heaven's consequent provision or refusal of a means to obtain the transfer.

The period from the fifth to the third centuries B.C. saw the first flowering of China's intellectual activities and the formulation of ethical, political and scientific theories that were destined to shape much of China's future thought. According to one theory, which was evolved at about 300 B.C., the creation of the world and the continued processes of nature were to be attributed to the complementary powers of the two major forces of *Yin* and *Yang*. The different impact of these two forces could be recognised in the everyday phenomena of the world. *Yin* was associated with female, dark and cold, *Yang* with male, light and heat; and the rhythmical procession of natural phenomena depended on which of the two forces happened to be in the ascendant. *Yin* and *Yang* were manifested in types of energy or qualities, or in the material elements of fire, water, metal, wood and earth whose creation they had contrived, but which were themselves powerful enough to ordain the form of the material world.

In the Han period there were perhaps thinkers who were ready to explain the world in these terms, resolutely refusing to ascribe its creation to the will of supernatural agencies. But at the same time the doctrine of *Yin-Yang* and the five elements had given rise to considerably less rationalist thought, and had left a lasting influence on contemporary artistic expression. The powers of the five elements became associated with other sets of objects or qualities that could be numbered in five, such as the colours (red, black, white, green and yellow) or the directions (south, north, west, east and centre). There were likewise five sacred mountains, five senses of human perception, five musical notes, not to speak of the five fingers of the hand and the five toes of the foot.

It had become fashionable to believe that the proper state of man on earth depended on maintaining the correct balance between the forces of *Yin* and *Yang*, and that the powers of certain members of the five elements, colours or directions could be engaged as allies against the dangers of natural disruption or even political disturbance. These ideas were introduced into some of the conventions and prescriptions of court protocol, and permeated the dynasty's faith in its own legitimate authority. Han sovereignty was explained as representing the dominant element of water, or later earth, and the appropriate colours were chosen for ceremonial use and display. At times of a *coup d'état* it could be maintained that the champion of a new political force stood for that one of the elements which was naturally due to rise to a position of ascendency in accordance with the terms of the cosmic rhythm. The champion would thus claim that he was acting in support of the natural order of the

39 The union of the two forces of *Yin* and *Yang* is symbolised by human figures with linked serpent-like tails. The figure on the left holds up the moon, and that on the right the sun; a hare appears on the moon and a bird on the sun

40 The Red Bird symbol of the south. From a cave-tomb

world and that it was the duty of all men who respected law and order to place their loyal support at his disposal.

It was a short step to propagate these ideas in association with omens that had been recently reported from different parts of the empire and which could be alleged to herald the emergence of one of the five elements in its rightful situation. The use of these doctrines for political purposes forms excellent evidence of the hold that they had on the minds of the leaders of Han China and the force which they could be hoped to exert on the minds of the led.

The same conclusion is to be drawn from the prevalence of the *Yin-Yang* and five-element motif as symbols in contemporary art forms and their appearance in religious observances. Tombs were laid out so as to conform with the concept of the five directions, guarded by the appropriate animals used symbolically. The symbolism is seen most conspicuously in the designs of bronze mirrors, which are in many ways the most characteristic products of Han artists. Some of these highly intricate designs have been explained as showing a circular universe which encloses a square earth. This was the home of the central direction and of yellow, surrounded on each side by the symbols of the other four elements and colours. Each side enjoyed its rightful season and was protected by its own guardian beast. According to the design, the full force of *Yin* appears in the north; it is dominant in winter and supported by the black warrior. It is manifested in black and thrives on water. On the opposite quadrant of the circle, *Yang* is in the ascendant attended by the red bird and glorying in the summer, in fire and in red. Similar symbols of the series are displayed in the other two quadrants, and it is clear from the imagery of the centre that the design sprang from a yearning to secure the earthly blessing of sons and grandsons, by harnessing the support of *Yin*, *Yang* or their acolyte creations.

At the same time the *Yin-Yang* and five-element motif may be combined with a means of attaining a state of immortality in a realm that lies apart from this world. The white tiger, symbol of metal and guardian of the west, sometimes leads the way to a heavenly world over which the Queen Mother of the West presides; and sometimes there are depicted winged dragons which can act as steeds to waft a man from this world to a life of immortal bliss. Other artistic designs portray the union of *Yin* and *Yang*, from which all creation derived.

Many imperial edicts bear witness to the force of these beliefs and to the service paid thereto by the government. Occasionally, important results ensued, such as the despatch of a large-scale and expensive expedition into Central Asia in 102 B.C.; one of the reasons for this may have been to satisfy the emperor's desire to acquire the heavenly steeds which he hoped would convey him to the land of the immortals. According to a later writer, the same emperor had had his masons so contrive the stonework of an ornamental tower that it would catch the dew which was believed to possess similarly efficacious properties. Unseasonal freaks of weather or the strange behaviour of the heavenly bodies which were reported to the

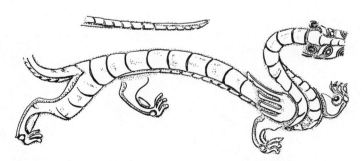

41 The White Tiger, the west's symbol. Figures *41–3* were carved on a coffin to avert evil influences. An inscription on the fourth side dates the grave at A.D. 221

throne could be utilised for political ends, perhaps somewhat unscrupulously.

A further technique practised by experts in the occult which engaged the attention of the highest in the land concerned the claim to foretell a man's destiny by examining his bodily features and interpreting these in the light of superhuman skills. Somebody once described the cast of features of Wang Mang, who displaced the Han house and ruled as emperor from A.D. 9 to 23. The terms used were far from commendatory. 'He can be said to have the eyes of an owl, the jowl of a tiger and the bark of a jackal. Yes, he's certainly capable of devouring others, but the chances are that he'll be devoured himself.' This frank forecast cost the unwary fortune-teller his life; but Wang Mang was sufficiently impressed by the event to exclude unknown or potentially dangerous visitors from close audiences.

Some of these religious or superstitious urges are revealed in the burial habits of Han China. These were by no means uniform, and allowances must be made for differences between the graves of the rich and the poor—of the leaders of society and the led; and between those that followed earlier styles and those where innovations were introduced. Most of the information at our disposal concerns the tombs prepared for the wealthier members of society who had passed their lives in the provinces of the interior.

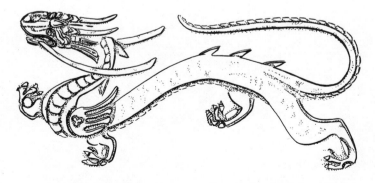

42 The Green Dragon, guardian symbol of the east

Originally graves had been dug as pits or shafts, but from the Han period there arose the custom of building special tombs of brick or stone, and the archaeologist's spade has revealed a large number of these structures. In the natural conditions of the south-west tunnel-graves were sometimes hewn in the living rock; while the use of the more simple pit-graves survived during the Han period in the south and the far north.

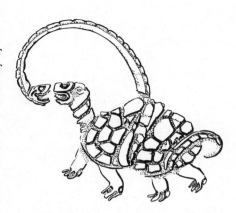

43 The Snake and Tortoise, symbol of the north

Many of the brick or stone tombs were surmounted by far more than a mere sprinkling of soil. One of the ways of making an ostentatious display in Han society was to pile a hillock over the tomb, so that it would rise aloft as a monument and landmark. The practice was severely criticised during the first century B.C., but the imperial family was itself one of the worst offenders. Up to 1956 it was still reported that the surviving traces of the emperor Wu ti's mausoleum (died 87 B.C.) rose to a height of some 30 metres. The planting of small ornamental copses was a further form of extravagance at an ancestor's tomb. But the principal way of honouring the deceased was to build a noble edifice, whose entrance was flanked by imposing towers and which was laid out in a series of chambers, passageways and shrines. The structure was often executed in large bricks, on which decorative designs had been embossed; sometimes stone was used, and massive pillars were clothed with a wealth of carving. Guardian beasts fashioned from stone blocks were occasionally placed at the entrance, and inscribed tablets declared to posterity the achievements of the deceased on earth.

There were doubtless many funerals which inspired the attendance of mourners who were sincerely moved by the occasion, and who genuinely desired to show their respect for a well-loved or much-honoured figure. In A.D. 200 the great scholar and teacher Cheng Hsüan died at the age of 74. Some of his former pupils had duly served in the government and risen to senior posts such as that of governor of a commandery; and with their junior colleagues they crowded to attend their master's obsequies, dressed in mourning garb. But, as we shall see (p. 142), some two and a half centuries previously a critic had complained bitterly of the hypocrisy of the times, when a man could not bring himself to serve his parents whilst they were living, but strove to win a reputation for proper feelings by the wealthy furnishings that he provided for their funerals.

When burials were made directly into a pit-grave the Chinese had used an outer and an inner coffin. In the Han tombs of brick or stone the vault itself did duty as the outer coffin and an inner wooden shell housed the corpse. The parts of this coffin were fastened by tenon joints and later with iron pins. The planks were cut from the choicest of woods and were richly decorated with paint or lacquer.

For the Han period we have examples of joint graves which housed the bodies of a man and his wife, or, occasionally, a man

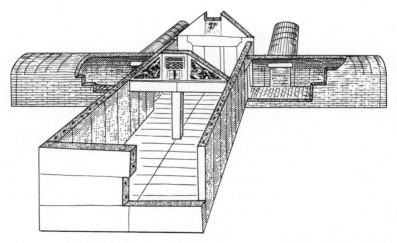

44 Plan of a brick tomb found near Lo-yang. It comprised two main chambers and two side rooms. The richly decorated panels of red, gold, green and purple, show well known moral stories and emblems of felicity. The triangular tableau separating the two chambers measures 206 by 86 cm.

and a child who had predeceased his parents. The sacrifice of animal or human victims to accompany the departed in the future life was now rarely practised, and in the place of this gruesome habit there had arisen the custom of providing the dead with the material equipment that they might need in the life beyond the grave. To this splendid gift to posterity, archaeologists and historians owe much of their knowledge of life in Han China; of the houses, granaries and water-wells; of a man's or woman's valuables, or of the furnishings and ornaments which they proudly possessed; of the carriages deemed suitable for the use of an official in the new society which he was entering. Wooden horses or clay manikins were interred so as to wait on their master or mistress; and the critic whom we have already met observed that while there were living creatures of the earth who lacked raiment, the puppets that accompanied the dead were clothed in the finest of silks. The walls of the tombs were sometimes gaily painted with scenes of happy occasions to which the man or his spouse could look back with some nostalgia; such as the dances or musical entertainments which they had promoted; the banquets that they had enjoyed; or the excursions on which they had spent their days of leisure.

For the poorer members of society pit burials were sufficient with their stark simplicity; and many a body was probably laid to rest in an earthenware shell. In times of famine or distress many corpses may have received no burial and lain about the roads or fields as a prey to wild beasts. Sometimes official steps were taken to collect these remains for disposal, so that a modicum of decency would be preserved. We may contrast the epitaph inscriptions of officials with those made to record the last resting place of convicts. For officials the characters were engraved with careful attention to calligraphic effect, and each inscription was composed as a piece of literature. The surviving slabs from a convicts' cemetery are covered in roughly scrawled characters, stating, for example: 'Here lie the remains of Chou Yang, of the prefecture of Wan in the commandery of Nan-yang, sentenced to building and guard duty without bodily mutilation; died on the 25th day of the 5th month in the 10th year of *Yung-yüan* [corresponding with 12 July A.D. 98].'

In addition to the cults which are described above, a further set of religious beliefs and practices which was evolving during the later part of the Han period is usually described under the term Taoism. The word *Tao* occurs in early Chinese writings and is usually translated as Way, Method or Principle. According to writers of the fifth and fourth centuries B.C., whose works are known to us as the *Tao-te-ching* and the *Chuang-tzu*, the *Tao* was the secret whereby the whole universe and its workings could be understood, and whereby an individual could best comply with its rhythmical processes. The principle soon ac-

45 Brick-work passage in a tomb near Lo-yang

quired social and political applications, but in its origin it is best understood as a mystical concept, born of the creative imagination of a few intellects. As such it must be sharply distinguished from Taoist religion, which grew up from entirely different motives, but which came to be associated with the authors of Taoist mysticism.

Taoist religion is more akin to the beliefs such as those which concerned a search for immortality and the use of intermediaries. There were men who claimed to possess a secret understanding of such matters, or to provide material blessings such as the cure of disease or the provision of rain. Religious practices followed when these masters of the occult were able to persuade their followers to carry out preliminary rites or offer supplications; and it could always be argued that if such efforts were rewarded by the desired blessing, this was due to the master's understanding of the way or to his secret powers; while a failure could be ascribed to the scepticism of those partaking in the ceremonies. Some masters demanded a material consideration for their devotions and tended to increase the mystery of their calling by adding greater solemnity

to the occasions. They administered potions to the patients who
sought their services, and had them adopt postures of atone-
ment for their faults whilst reciting prayers or incantations.
Sometimes charms were made out bearing the name of the
patient and offered respectively to Heaven, Earth and Water;
and the association of these practices with the *Tao* or Way of the
earlier mystical writers was confirmed by invocations to Lao
Tzu, reputedly the author of the *Tao-te-ching* and master of the
Way itself.

These cults took over many esoteric practices that were
already current. The Taoist priests would invoke the spirits
of the departed and seek to restore them to life in the person
of a medium. Trance and ecstasy, dietary regulation and control of the breath were some of the devices utilised to render the
body the master rather than servant of death. The emergence
of a Taoist church with its disciplines and dignitaries, its
festivals, fasts and sacred texts is of profound importance to the
development of religious practice in China; and although the
organisation of these communities cannot be dated until after
the Han period, many of the constituent elements were already
present in late Han society.

The arrival of the faith of the Buddha in China must be set
against a social and cultural background which included an
age-old belief in the spirits of nature, Heaven and ancestors,
a search to evade death, and an understanding of the world in
terms of elemental forces and their symbols. It is uncertain
when the propagators of Buddhism first arrived in China;
according to the well-known official account the faith was
revealed to the emperor Ming ti in a visionary dream in about
A.D. 65, and there are some anecdotes which refer to an earlier
arrival. Probably word had been passed by merchants or other
travellers who brought their wares from northern India across
the hills and deserts of Central Asia. This process probably took
place between about 50 B.C. and A.D. 50.

At first the faith was practised by foreigners who had settled
in Han territory; and perhaps the earliest authentic record of
Chinese participation is a short reference to the 'gentle sacrifices
to the Buddha' that were performed by a member of the imperial family in about A.D. 65. By about 100 or earlier the

religion had become more generally accepted at the capital city of Lo-yang, where the work of translating the Sanksrit scriptures into Chinese was soon to begin (from about A.D. 150). Shortly before A.D. 200 we hear of a temple which had been founded on Chinese initiative near Hsia-p'ei (modern Kiangsu province). It was furnished with a brazen statue, with a gilt covering and silken robes; and the building was possibly built of several storeys, with a central shaft or steeple. The temple could accommodate large congregations of those who came to listen to the scriptures, and the devout were entertained with ceremonies and refreshment. Meanwhile up at Lo-yang the name of the Buddha was being coupled with that of Lao Tzu, allegedly the author of the *Tao-te-ching*, in sacrifices which the emperor performed in 166.

Buddhism was now becoming a religion of the Chinese people as well as of the alien sojourners, but we do not know how widespread was its appeal, or how accustomed the Han Chinese had become to its imagery, priests and ceremonies. The faith rested on the belief that human suffering can be avoided by the renunciation of desires, and rules of behaviour were prescribed to attain that perfect state of non-suffering. While Taoism rested largely on the practice of techniques that were aimed at preserving the body as a home fit for the soul, Buddhists hoped to free both body and soul from the pain of this world. This ideal state of salvation could be achieved by any individual, and the practice of the faith might in this way cut across notions of higher or lower stations in home or state. As yet the faith was not sufficiently well-established to conflict critically with established ideas, and there had not been time to realise the social and economic implications of the communal life of a monastery.

The Han people were thus subject to the call of a whole variety of spiritual exercises and requirements. It was not for nothing that those who trusted to the personal teachings of Confucius needed to stress repeatedly the value of moral principles and the need of a disciplined mode of behaviour to regulate the relations of the individual, the home and the state. A moralist and rationalist reaction was only to be expected in the prevailing mood of ignorance, superstition and gullibility. It is perhaps not surprising that Han historians and other writers chose to recount the noble deeds of ancient heroes so as to stress the need to aid humanity; and the artists whose mark yet remains on the walls of Han tombs sometimes took as their subject those anecdotes which would best illustrate a man's duty to his parents or the value of a just and kindly government to mankind.

10

The capital city
of Ch'ang-an

The greater part of the Han population was engaged in agriculture, and there is no means of determining what proportion
lived in the towns as courtiers or officials, tradesmen or artisans,
coolies or beggars. Some scholars take the view that as much as
a third of the population were townsmen—almost 18 million
souls; and a more conservative estimate of a tenth would still
imply that in A.D. 1–2 China included sufficient towns to house
some six million individuals.

But whatever the strength of the urban population and
whatever the number of towns in Han China, we can be sure
that they were distributed irregularly up and down the provinces and that they differed markedly in size. Many towns
were probably not new foundations so much as extensions built
on or near the sites of much older settlements; and the choice of
situation depended on natural features such as an assured
supply of water, or strong defences. In so far as each of the 1500
prefectures of A.D. 1–2 provided a seat of administration for the
prefect, they can be said to have included at least one 'town',
but many prefectures in the populous areas must have included
several settlements, which were arising to serve a variety of
purposes. For the Han town was not only an administrative
centre; it supplied a market-place and acted as a centre of communications; and sometimes it housed a military headquarters.
In addition, Han China had its mining towns and its cities
which earned their living by weaving textiles, working metals or
exploiting the salt industry.

The lists of the administrative units which comprised the
empire in A.D. 1–2 include figures for the inhabitants of ten

prefectures only. These were perhaps inserted somewhat exceptionally in the case of highly prosperous and important centres whose size was deemed worthy of record, and the ten examples cannot be taken as typical. Of the ten, Ch'ang-an and Lo-yang acted as the empire's capital from 202 B.C. to A.D. 8 and from A.D. 25 to 220 respectively; Ch'eng-tu, in the west country, was the largest and P'eng-ch'eng the smallest of the other eight. The figures,* of which examples follow, may refer to the population of the surrounding rural parts of the administrative areas as well as the cities themselves. According to one scholar a realistic estimate of the number of persons who resided within the walls of Ch'ang-an at this time would be nearer 80,000 than the quarter of a million that is given.

city	households	individuals
Ch'ang-an	80,000	246,200
Lo-yang	52,839	[195,504]
Ch'eng-tu	76,256	[282,147]
P'eng-ch'eng	40,196	[148,725]

The choice of Ch'ang-an or Lo-yang as the site for the capital city depended partly on strategic and economic considerations and partly on a desire to associate the ruling house with earlier incidents of China's history. From Han times on, until the tenth century, one of these two cities was usually adopted as the capital by the dynasties seated in the north of China.

Long before the imperial period cities had been built with two sets of fortifications. One set enclosed the other, and the city was envisaged as a rectangle. In the Han cities of Ch'ang-an and Lo-yang a formal design was perhaps imposed on the natural lines of a developing city, so as to symbolise the ideal regularity of the imperial order and the view of society as a series of interrelated groups, each placed in its own rightful position in the universe.

The material remains of Han Ch'ang-an corroborate many

---

* These are mostly given as exact figures. Round figures, as for Ch'ang-an, may be an early approximation. Figures for the individuals are not always given in the text; the estimates given here in parenthesis have been calculated on the basis of the average size of the household at 3·7 members.

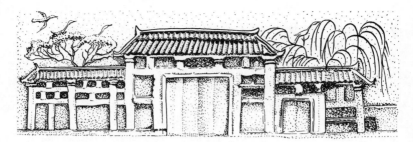

46 The frontage of a residence showing the tops of trees growing inside the court

statements of the traditional literary sources. The city was built to face the south, so that, when seated in his audience chamber, the emperor also faced the south; for that direction was the domain of the *Yang* and marked the sun's uppermost position in the heavens. While the eastern wall of the city ran directly from north to south, the walls on the other three sides were not quite so regular, though they followed the directions of the compass. The total distance round the walls amounted to over 25 kilometres, and each of the four sides was pierced by three imposing gateways. These allowed access by three separate entrances, each of which measured six metres in width. Traces of ruts left by a vehicle show that each entrance could admit four carriages simultaneously. The roads which led into the city from the gates were laid out in three parallel tracks which corresponded with the positions of the three entrances.

Much of the original Han city was destroyed in fighting and fires during the disturbed periods of A.D. 9–27 and 190–5, and not one of the dynastic houses which adopted Ch'ang-an as its capital in the next four centuries was able to rebuild it in a manner that was comparable with its former glory. Only when the Sui (589–617) and T'ang (618–906) dynasties arose was the city restored to its earlier splendour; but by then the site of the settlement had been shifted; and the noble city which served as a capital from the seventh century lay to the south-east of the area when Han Ch'ang-an had been erected.

Although the decision to establish the seat of government at Ch'ang-an was taken in 202 B.C., the work of building the protecting walls was not started until 194. Within the next four years large forces of labourers were assigned to this task. These were presumably men who had been called up for their statutory duty of a month's service annually. They were drawn from fairly distant parts of China, and the histories specify that women as well as men were employed on the work. Surviving monuments to their labours measure 16 metres wide at the base; but as the walls were tapered at an angle of 11° the width at the top must have been less. The walls were built of stamped earth and some bricks. The 12 gates were furnished with watch-towers to enable the superintendents to keep a look-out and close the city gates if the situation so demanded. The city was perhaps traversed by boulevards running from east to west and north to south, with earthenware gullies at the side to drain away the water. Possibly these streets served to divide the whole area into wards, some of which could be set aside as sites for palaces, quarters for visitors or, towards the end of the Han period, for a Buddhist establishment. But most of the 160 wards which allegedly existed were used for residential purposes, with dwellings lying packed together 'as closely as the teeth of a comb', as a contemporary poet once put it.

There were several market-places in Ch'ang-an which were said to have formed meeting grounds for travellers who came from many parts of Asia. A sharp watch was kept on the conduct of transactions by officials who were specially appointed to supervise conditions of trading. A notable writer of the first century A.D. looked back with some degree of poetic licence to the heyday of Ch'ang-an's prosperity, when the markets were so full of goods and people that there was no room for a man to turn his head, let alone for a waggon to face about. In addition to trade, the market-places were used for other purposes, e.g., the practice of divination; and they formed the scene of more gruesome spectacles, such as the public execution of traitors

47 Clay model of a house found near the modern city of Canton

or fallen statesmen. Thus it came about that Ch'ao Ts'o met a violent end at the hands of the axemen in the Eastern Market, in 154 B.C. The incident served to underline the strong and ruthless nature of imperial government; to warn potential criminals of the terrible fate that might await them; and to appease the anger of Ch'ao Ts'o's political opponents.

Unfortunately we cannot altogether trust some of the literary accounts which purport to refer to the Han city of Ch'ang-an. Such sources were based on a variety of information and rested partly on the author's imagination; and the descriptive details may well refer to a state of civilisation that was reached long after the Han period. But whatever the exaggeration it is likely that the imperial palaces were built with the greatest attention to the luxury and comfort of their residents; without overmuch care for expense; and with full use of the skills of artists and craftsmen.

There were several palaces erected at different times in response to an emperor's mood, or to house a member of the imperial family. Each palace probably comprised one or more audience halls, flanked by separate towers and gateways, and later sources describe the extravagance of the material used and the rich standard of artistry. But it was perhaps not for some centuries after the Han period that the imperial residences were built with special winter quarters that were equipped with fire-screens and cosy wrappings, and with the Pure Cool quarters that were constantly freshened by fans and ice in the summer. The ascription of these comforts to the Han emperors cannot be accepted without further evidence.

The palaces must have presented a sharp contrast with most of the buildings of the city, whose construction was of a very humble standard. Even the palace buildings were not always built of brick or stone, and some of the walls were made of clay and wattle, covered in plaster and brightly painted scarlet and white. The gateways were perhaps the most imposing parts of the buildings, with their towers placed symmetrically to enclose the entrances and to house the upper chambers of the guardsmen. While thatch may well have been the usual form of roofing material, tiles were laid on the halls and chambers of the emperors. These were moulded in earthenware as half-cylinders; and when they were laid side by side in lines the rain-water would drain away in the valleys that lay between adjacent tiles. At the lower end of the roof the half-cylinder was sealed with a rounded tile-end which could be used to carry artistic or propagandist designs.

There are many surviving examples of these circular medallions, which formed an admirable medium for a calligrapher to demonstrate his skill. Some roundels bear the name of the palace of which they formed part; others carry a short invocation for eternal bliss; and on some specimens the artist traced a stag or a bird as a decorative device. Interesting examples of a propagandist use of the roundel come from sites lying near China's northern borders, where contacts had been made with foreign peoples and Chinese defensive forts had been built. A passer-by whose glance fell on the tiles could read that 'Heaven has brought about the foreigners' submission' or 'All aliens submit'.

Many a tale is told of the glories of Han Ch'ang-an; of the imperial pleasure gardens that lay beyond the west wall, stocked with botanical rarities from the south and strange beasts from different climes. There are highly imaginative details of the landscaping of this park, of the ornamental towers with which it was studded and the lakes contrived for pleasure. We are also told of the many towers that had been built within the city walls, some for religious purposes, some to facilitate observation of the heavenly bodies or the phenomena produced by the *Yin* and the *Yang*; and as the beings of the immortal world were thought to be fond of towered buildings, Wu ti is said to have erected several in Ch'ang-an as a means of attracting their favours.

We are perhaps on firmer ground in respect of some of the religious buildings of the Han city. There was a *Ming-t'ang*, or Hall of Brilliance which was intimately connected with the ceremonies that assured the dynasty its survival and whose construction was a matter of learned speculation and controversy among the scholars of the day. There were the ancestral shrines devoted to the emperor's ancestors; and we are told that in the shrine of Kao tsu the founder, there were hanging a set of four or ten bells, of immense size and capable of deep reverberation. But here perhaps our account is less reliable, as the

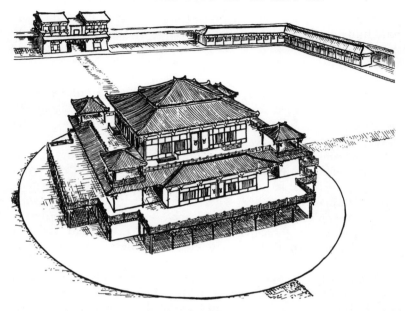

48 Reconstruction of a ceremonial building, based on archaeological finds near Ch'ang-an. The central structure faced due north and consisted of four main halls, each with an outer covered terrace. The surrounding square of four walls, each measuring 235 metres in length, was built with four central gateways and with auxiliary buildings at each corner. A circular moat marked the outer perimeter of the area. Probably built in the Western Han period

author may have been thinking of bells that hung in later ages in the temples and monasteries of the Buddhist faith.

Services were held at the principal shrines at appointed seasons of the year, and it was in these solemn surroundings that the emperor received the annual homage and tribute from the marquises of the realm (see p. 57). Similarly, when the kings were invested with their authority the ceremony took place in the presence of the emperor's ancestors. South of the city the emperor worshipped Heaven at a circular altar, placed in the quarter where the *Yang* was dominant. For the worship of Earth a square altar was sited in the north, where the *Yin* exerted its greatest powers.

Recent excavations have revealed traces of a set of Han buildings that were used for ceremonial or religious purposes.

There is reason to believe that the central feature consisted of a hall built in three storeys and raised on a low platform, and that this was enclosed by a square arcade. This was constructed with four gateways which were set to face the points of the compass and in which ancillary buildings nestled; and the perimeter of the site was formed by a continuous circular ditch. The plan of the site bears a marked resemblance to the designs seen on some of the bronze mirrors of the Han period whose symbolism has been discussed above (see p. 118).

Two depositories of documents within the city were said to have been built by a statesman who had played a vital role in founding the dynasty and acted as its principal servant of state until his death in 193 B.C. In the civil wars which had preceded the foundation of the Han house, this statesman had taken steps to preserve intact the records of the previous administration, with the result that the new government could start its work with the help of its predecessor's maps, and, possibly, its tax returns. These records were deposited in a stone-built chamber that still stored such documents a century or two later.

It was in the second depository, the Pavilion of the Blessings of Heaven, that Liu Hsiang is said to have worked on his project of collating and cataloguing the texts of the imperial library in about 25 B.C. (see p. 98). If a charming anecdote can be believed, as he worked there one evening wrapped in concentration, an elderly stranger, wearing yellow robes and leaning

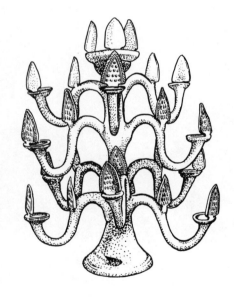

49 An earthen-ware lamp-stand made to hold twelve lights, found in a tomb of A.D. 182 in the modern province of Ho-pei

on a freshly cut staff, knocked on the door and saw him sitting and reading in the failing light. The stranger breathed on the tip of his staff, which burst into flame; so he shone a light for Liu Hsiang, and began to expound the mysteries of the five elements, and to explain the difficulties in one of the classical texts. Liu Hsiang was afraid that he would forget the long lecture, but he had no spare material on which to write; so he tore strips of silk from his gown to record the words as they were spoken. When dawn broke and he asked the stranger for his name, he revealed that he was no mortal being, but a spirit sent from Heaven to inspect the standard of the Liu's scholarship of which so much had been heard and to assist in its advancement.

Beyond the confines of the city were a few named granaries and stables. Some of the bridges that took travellers across the river Wei were said to be built of stone; and away across the north bank lay the imperial graves in sites which were scrupulously chosen for each occasion to make sure that their masters would be protected from the hazards and baleful influences of the world.

50 Tile-end (see p. 133, and figure 37). The half-cylinder is closed with a roundel, bearing four characters that mean 'Long happiness without end'. (The top of the tile has been decorated and remodelled in recent times)

Life in the cities

For some 80 years after the foundation of the Han empire in 202 B.C. the government's policy was aimed at consolidation rather than advance. Statesmen were bent on strengthening the authority of the imperial house and on promoting the efficiency of the central administration. Foreign policy was as yet defensive and negative, and the emphasis of the exchequer was placed on retrenchment and the harbouring of resources. But from about 120 B.C. a change set in; the government tried to plan how the efforts of its subjects could be best spent, and to make sure that the working activities of man-power were being directed to the most suitable objectives. Statesmen were anxious to see that the work of the fields was being maintained simultaneously with the increasing efforts spent in the mines and foundries, or in the exchange and transport of goods; and if fortunes were to be made from such undertakings the government wished to take a due share of the profits. This change accompanied a new view of foreign affairs which allowed for expansion and the deployment of conscripts so as to set up and protect the trade-routes that stretched into Central Asia.

Although the new policies met with some conspicuous successes there were several occasions in the ensuing decades when the plans of the new school of statesmen were brought into question. One of the best known reviews of policy took place in 81 B.C., following an imperial edict which ordered an investigation of the causes of popular distress. The statesmen and their consultants interpreted their terms of reference very widely, and proceeded to review the principles that lay behind the government's planning and the wisdom of certain measures of control that had been adopted. One of the most fascinating documents of the Han age is an account of these deliberations that was probably written a decade or two after the event.

The debate of 81 B.C. was conducted by successive pairs of disputants representing alternately the government and the critics, and corresponding very generally to the progressive and the conservative elements at Ch'ang-an. It is easy to see that the account is by no means a verbatim record, and we find that the conservative critic is always given the last word, with his opponent reduced to silence. But the propagandist flavour of the document does not necessarily detract from its value, however much it seems to be special pleading. The conservative spokesmen rail against the state of society that had been built as a result of the progressives' policies, and their strictures draw on a description of the imbalances and injustices of town life. They compare the contemporary affluence with the thrift of their forbears, and they allude to the practices of the very rich, the well-to-do and the poorer sections of Han society. There is a strong ring of truth in these descriptions; in the technical expressions and the allusions to marketing terms. But although the description of town life which follows can be taken as realistic there is no means of assessing the extent to which its extravagances were practised. We do not know what proportion of Ch'ang-an's population could afford the luxuries that are so bitterly decried or what particular section of the community was the critics' target. It is very likely that not many inhabitants of the city could indulge their fancies in the manner which could evidently not command universal approval.

Opulent families lived in multi-storeyed houses, built with intersecting cross-beams and rafters that were richly carved and decorated on all visible surfaces. The stairways and partitions were plastered or painted. Instead of the simple skins or grass-made mats on which their ancestors had been content to rest, these families covered their floors with embroidered cushions, woollen rugs or rush-mats trimmed to a nicety; and even middle-class families could afford to take their ease on coverings of wild boar hide or the smooth felts that came from the north. In the inner rooms of the house the beds were carefully furnished with wooden fittings cut from the choicest

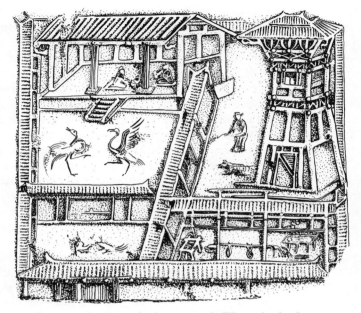

51 Panoramic view of a homestead. The principal quarters
on the left are reached through two courtyards. The
domestic offices are separate, lying to the right and including
a kitchen with tables and a wooden frame for hanging food
and utensils. Beside the watch-tower a servant sweeps the
courtyard and a dog is tethered

timber; fine embroideries were hung up as drapes, and screens
were set to overlap each other and ensure privacy.

There was a shocking profusion of fine silk among the rich.
Even ordinary folk donned the sort of garments that were fit for
queens, and everyday wear was bright enough for weddings.
While the wealthier classes wore choice furs of squirrel or fox,
and wild duck plumes, others were content with woollens and
ferret skins. The same was true of footwear, with affluent
members of society sporting shoes of inlaid leather or silk-lined
slippers. But the worst excesses of dress were associated with
weddings, when you could see the rich classes with their red
badger furs and their tinkling jades; and even the well-to-do
could afford long skirts, with jewels, clasps and earrings.

The critics protested vigorously against the extravagant habits of the age which formed such a sharp contrast with the frugality of earlier generations. Game was now taken out of season indiscriminately, and young fish or fledglings were trapped without a thought for the stock, to be enjoyed with leeks, ginger or other seasonings. In the past, wine and meat had appeared only at festivals, and even the nobility had refused to slaughter animals for food without due cause; but in contemporary society meat could always be seen hanging up for sale in town or country alike. Nowadays it was quite a common thing at a banquet to be regaled with one dish after another, with roasts and minced fish; kid, quails and oranges; pickles and other relishes. The same story could be told of the rows of cooked-meat stalls in the markets. What a difference there was between the indolence of men who were supposed to be at work and the eagerness with which they hurried to buy their piglets, dog-cutlets or chopped liver, their broth or their roasts. Needless to say these delicacies were not served in the earthenware or wooden vessels which had done duty in the past. Only the best of cups would suffice, fashioned with silver inlay or with golden handles.

Naturally the rich families needed adequate means of transport up and down Ch'ang-an's streets, and you could see their carriages drawn up in rows, gleaming in silver or gold and fitted with every sort of gadget. The horses themselves were neatly decked and shod, and caparisoned with breast-plates and pendant jewellery. They were kept in check by means of gilt or painted bits, with golden or inlaid bridles;

52 A musician playing a half-tube zither with three strings and three pegs. This player forms one of a team of four instrumentalists and with figures 53–4 and 57–8 comes from a richly decorated tomb in East China. Although a little after the Han period, the scenes of entertainment are probably little different from those of Han times

53 A pan-pipes player, one of an orchestral section of five. The line across the pipes represents the method of attaching them together

and the not-so-rich made do with lacquered leather equipment or tassels. With these extravagances there should be borne in mind the comparative cost of keeping the horses alive, as a single animal consumed as much grain as an ordinary family of six members.

There was no shortage of entertainments for the rich, who would amuse themselves looking at performing animals, tiger-fights and foreign girls. Musical performances were no longer restricted to special occasions such as folk festivals and the tunes and dances were far more sophisticated than they had been in the past. Rich families now kept their own five-piece orchestras with bells and drums, and their house-choirs; and the middle-rich arranged their flute or lyre concerts, sometimes with a visiting artiste who came from central or eastern China.

The strength of religious beliefs and practices and their effect on daily life was a further reason for dismay. There was altogether too much devotion to strange powers or spirits, with animal sacrifices, musical shows and puppetry. Very often these rites were performed simply to secure an earthly happiness from the supernatural powers, and without any attention to moral standards or the decencies of human conduct. People were gullible, trusting to luck and open to any sort of tricks, provided that they held out a hope of material improvement; and a serious devotion to duty had often been replaced by attention to the occult.

Ostentation and hypocrisy were particularly noticeable in the attentions paid to the dead. People used the finest of woods for

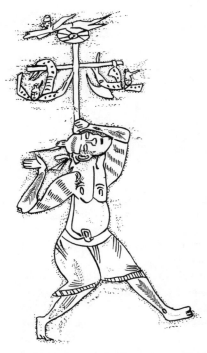

54 Juggling: two child acrobats perform on the horizontal bar and a third revolves on the wheel at the top of the pole, which is supported by a juggler whose arms and legs are bare

the coffin, and even the poor managed to get the lids painted. A wealth of equipment was interred with the corpse, whose resting place was marked by mounds, groves and towers. Of course, a funeral formed an excellent pretext for a communal repast, and the mourners were entertained with singing, dancing and play-acting. The diatribe continues:

Of old when a man served his living parents he did so with his full love, and when he followed their bones on their last journey he did so with unmitigated grief. So the Holy Leaders of old drew up regulations to prevent the senseless elaboration of these practices. But now, while their parents are still alive, sons cannot bring it upon themselves to render them the love and obedience that is their due; but once a parent dies, the children vie with one another in their extravagances. They may have no feelings of grief, but by virtue of the luxurious funeral and the rich furnishings that they provide so will they win a name for fulfilling their duties. Their reputation will stand out among their contemporaries and their fine deeds will become a matter of common knowledge; and we then find ordinary members of the public imitating the ways of the rich and ruining themselves in the process.

The critics of the government of 81 B.C. were disturbed at the misdirection of working effort, often for projects which had no intrinsic interest and which were designed for show. Meanwhile popular distress remained unrelieved and the fields were not worked to their full capacity. But there was always labour available to keep the government's stations in a good state of repair. Strange beasts and exotic creatures were being nurtured at official orders, but these were little use when it came to farm-work; and men who would have been far better employed at their ploughs were told off to look after these animals. Worst of all, while one could find human beings who were short of clothing or who had to live off the coarsest of foods, there were dogs and horses decked in the finest embroideries and animals raised on food fit for human consumption.

There was a shocking imbalance to be observed between different sections of the population. Government offices up and down the country maintained large numbers of slaves, of both sexes, who could draw official supplies of food and clothing without making a comparable return. They were able to engage in private enterprises to net their wicked gains, but they never worked to their utmost, and it was the government which forfeited the valuable services which they might have rendered. While ordinary members of the population had not even a peck of provisions in store, the slaves in government offices counted their gold pieces by the hundred; and while the peasantry had no respite from their labours by day or night, male and female slaves sat by with their hands folded. Finally

55 Clay model of a cook-
ing stove, found near Can-
ton. One of the vessels on
it is a steamer, and there is
an opening for fuel and a
chimney for the smoke

56 The game of *liu-po* was played by two opponents supported by seconds, and depended on the throw or manipulation of rods and counters and the use of a cup. The design of the pieces may have been associated with the symbolic beasts (figures *40–3*), and the powers of *Yin* and *Yang* (figure *39*)

there was the scandal of the idle immigrants, who came from both the north and the south. They gave no service to the community but enjoyed the best of material comforts, while the Chinese population toiled unceasingly for a mere pittance. It could hardly escape our critic that side by side with the palaces of Ch'ang-an and their noble parklands lay the slums and hovels of many of the city's inhabitants where no blade of grass could grow and no tree could flourish.

The critics were doubtless exaggerating the situation as they warmed to their task. However, many of the details which they describe recur in a tract written some two and a half centuries later by a somewhat disappointed man of affairs who had withdrawn from public life, and the essay perhaps serves to support these allegations of luxury and gay abandon. Wang Fu was writing from a somewhat different political outlook, and he was describing Lo-yang in place of Ch'ang-an; but he picks on much the same sort of evidence, enlarging on the waste of effort spent on playthings, and alluding with some asperity to those who lived by their wits or on their gains at gambling.

Betting for high stakes may have been frowned upon in the higher reaches of society, and we know of a few cases when men of superior social status may have been punished severely for the practice. For gambling was a means of taking money from one's fellow-men and of gaining wealth without making any contribution to the well-being of humanity. One game, called *Liu-po*, was probably played by two or four people. Six bamboo sticks, suitably marked with lines, were shaken out of a cup, like dice; and the throw probably entitled the player to move his counters on the board to carefully prescribed positions. The game was evidently accompanied by lively gestures and noisy shouts; and in addition to being the sport of men it is occasionally represented as a pastime of the immortals.

In the same essay Wang Fu castigates other extravagances. He had sharp words for the habit of cutting expensive coloured silks to form charms or amulets; and he deplored the way in which the general public had been deluded into trusting to witchcraft rather than physic to cure its bodily ills.

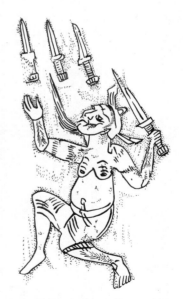

In addition to these literary pieces, material evidence in the form of the reliefs that decorated a tomb illustrates the type of entertainment that rich families could afford to stage, right at the end of the Han period. There was dancing and sword-play, juggling and acrobatic feats, accompanied by skilled players with their drums and bells, their wind and string instruments; and we know of other forms of amusement in Ch'ang-an or Lo-yang, such as cock-fighting, dog or horse racing and bird hunting.

But these delights were limited

57 This sword-juggler is bearded and wears shorts

to only a few of the many elements who made up Ch'ang-an's population. Ambitious men had come there from many parts of China intent on making their fortunes, and the city was attractive enough to those who pursued wealth, status or power and had little time for frivolities. Quite apart from the palace and the officials, the city housed a large population of families whose living conditions contrasted sharply with those of the houses which they served. The poorer members of society could easily become a prey to their more unscrupulous neighbours, who were strong enough to disregard the laws of government and to employ gangs who practised violence or oppression so as to achieve their ends.

From time to time the city suffered from a crime-wave and the efficient preservation of law and order depended very largely on the personality and strength of the senior officials. There were occasions when the governor resorted to trickery to effect the arrest of criminals; or else it may have been possible to overawe or bribe the rich leaders of the underworld so as to reduce the extent of murder, robbery and kidnapping. Officials themselves were sometimes open to corruption; indeed, one governor arranged for an increase in the pay of the city constables, so as to decrease the likelihood of bribery. We hear also

58 Two large clapperless bells are suspended from a decorated frame. The player strikes with an external hammer slung from a beam

of bands of ill-disciplined youths who roamed the city, wearing their own distinctive garb and protective armour, and carrying knives and other weapons with which to intimidate the inhabitants.

Thanks to the funerary furnishings found in many Han tombs we can gain some idea of the living quarters, at least of the wealthier members of society. Both the miniature clay houses themselves and the pictures modelled on decora-

59 Clay model of a granary from southern China

tive bricks can be taken to be realistic, and the great variety of replicas makes a general description impossible. Some of the larger establishments were four-sided, with a high surrounding wall. There would be a main entrance placed centrally in one side, flanked by decorative pillars and surmounted by a gatehouse. An extensive courtyard within may have been divided into an inner and outer part by a separating wall. Possibly the outer part was planted with shrubs or trees, and some models depict birds or animals disporting themselves there. There might be a drive leading to a gate or gates in the wall which separated the inner from the outer courtyard, and it was here that a visitor would dismount from his carriage to be admitted into the residence proper. In addition to the main living rooms, the estate included store-houses, a kitchen, pigsties and a lavatory.

There are models of houses built in one or two storeys, with an outside stairway and slits or flaps that did duty as windows. Rooms erected specifically for food-storage were sometimes raised on stilts, to keep the grain away from the damp and rats, but dwelling houses usually lay directly on the ground. The plan of a house was sometimes square, with three of its four quarters forming an L-shaped, two-storeyed structure, and the fourth part being left open, or roofed in above the ground floor.

Some houses were π-shaped, others were formed as long halls supported by a lean-to at each end; and the more complicated buildings were topped with an array of roofs that formed an intricate and formal geometrical pattern. The clay models often included signs of habitation, such as human figures at their daily tasks, or dogs that lay in their kennels or kept watch over the property. The roofs were made of tile with rather a low pitch. Inside, the wooden beams that supported the structure lay criss-cross over each other, to be polished, carved or painted as the master ordered.

One advantage of living in the capital city lay in the chance to learn about foreigners and their way of life. There were indeed many thousands of conscript soldiers who had seen service at the distant fronts and returned to their villages or towns to tell the tale of their adventures; but the more sophisticated accounts, which were doubtless no less colourful than those of the private soldier, came from the officers and colonists, the explorers or traders who had returned to Ch'ang-an or Lo-yang after the successful conclusion of their missions in Central or Southern Asia. There is little doubt that wild and exaggerated stories sometimes circulated in town regarding the mysterious ways of the westerner or the abundance of his material resources.

Sometimes the Chinese officials serving in the 'colonies' of Vietnam, Korea or elsewhere had made a personal contact with the leaders of the local communities and succeeded in persuading them to cooperate with the intruding Chinese in a friendly way. There were times when the loyalties of the tribesmen were bought for a price of Chinese manufactured silks; and occasionally these leaders were presented with the most signal mark of favour that a Chinese emperor could bestow, a seal and ribbon declaring that the holder possessed high rank in Chinese society. On other occasions these seals were conferred on alien leaders who came to visit the Han capital; and while such missions were housed in their special apartments, the local inhabitants of Ch'ang-an or Lo-yang could see for themselves something of the foreigner and his ways, as he strolled or drove around their city.

A contemporary poem may perhaps form a fitting conclusion

60 Ladle: red pottery, glazed

61 Cooking stove: earthenware model from a tomb, with impressions
of animals' heads, a fish and a kitchen implement (see also figure 55)

149

62 Bronze box. The design is comparable with that in figure *11*

to this brief glimpse of Han cities. The translation is by the late Arthur Waley.

Green, green,
The cypress on the mound.
Firm, firm,
The boulder in the stream.
Man's life lived within this world
Is like the sojourning of a hurried traveller.
A cup of wine together will make us glad,
And a little friendship is no little matter.

Yoking my chariot I urge my stubborn horses,
*I wander about in the streets of Wan and Lo.**
In Lo Town how fine everything is!
The 'Caps and Belts'† go seeking each other out.
The great boulevards are intersected by lanes,
Wherein are the town houses of Royal Dukes.
The two palaces stare at each other from afar,
The twin gates rise a hundred feet.
By prolonging the feast let us keep our hearts gay,
And leave no room for sadness to creep in.

* Nan-yang and Lo-yang, in the modern province of Honan.
† High-ranking officials.

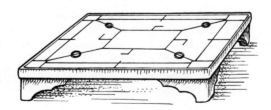

63 The markings on this reconstructed *liu-po* board may be related to the lines used for astronomical purposes on sundials (figure *33*), and some mirrors (figure *1*). The game may have been associated with divination

12

Trade and communications

The two centuries that preceded the establishment of the Ch'in and Han empires were marked by conspicuous changes in China's economy which had favoured the growth of city life and the development of a more highly sophisticated culture. Improved means of communication, a more extensive use of iron and a demand for luxury goods tended to promote the exchange of merchandise; and the attainment of political unification and stability under the empire enhanced the opportunities for profit-making by large-scale and small-scale operators alike.

A traditional bias against the tradesman had already been formulated before the Han period, from considerations of both theory and expediency. It was felt that the main working effort of humanity should properly be directed to extracting nature's gifts from the soil; and that, whereas such an occupation was honourable and praiseworthy, a merchant's business, which depended on squeezing a profit from his fellow human beings, was questionable and even shameful. But Han governments took a hand in controlling, and even expediting, trade for practical reasons. It was realised that society was coming more and more to depend on the work of specialists, and therefore on regular trading; and in some circles it was thought that if there were profits to be made from such undertakings they should be directed to the government's coffers and not into private hands. Some Han statesmen feared that the merchants would be ready to advance their own interests by whatever means they could, even to the extent of exploiting local shortages for the purpose. It therefore seemed right that the government should itself take some part in controlling the distribution of goods to ensure that this was being done on fair and reasonable terms. We therefore hear of attempts that were made to regulate the coinage, to set up state monopolies or to stabilise prices.

Cowry shells had formed the first medium of exchange in China. In the Bronze Age these had been superseded by bronze knives or shovels, which were both rarely found but of universal use, and acquired a recognised value for purposes of trade. Soon, small replicas took the place of the real articles, and in some parts of China there was evolved the disc coin, also cast from bronze. Under the Ch'in and Han dynasties a single circular coin formed the standard unit of currency. In the early days of the Han dynasty the minting of coin was not controlled, with the result that there was a variety of coins in circulation, from the heavy pieces of the old Ch'in mints to the light leaf-like coppers that private mine-owners were casting. From time to time the Han governments tried to impose a control on minting, and this was finally achieved in 112 B.C., with the adoption of the five-*shu* piece, and the restriction of its manufacture to government agencies.

The five-*shu* coin was so called after its inscription, which declared that its weight was five *shu* (corresponding with three grams). There was a square hole in the centre, so that units of a hundred coins could be strung together. In some issues a raised rim was cast at the edge of the coin or along the edge of the central hole to prevent clipping. In some of the coins issued before the adoption of the standard five-*shu* piece the lead content had been as high as 25 per cent; but thereafter there was a copper content of about 80 per cent, made up with tin, lead or iron. For major transactions, including those in which

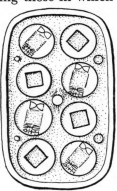

64 A mould used to mint five-*shu* coins. The inscription on the reverse side gives the name of the craftsman and the date of manufacture: 7th month, 2nd year of the reign-period *Keng-shih*, corresponding with August to September A.D. 24

65 The standard five-*shu* piece, regularly minted from 112 B.C.

the marquises presented their dues to the emperor, golden ingots sometimes changed hands; and there was a recognised value of 10,000 copper coins to the golden piece, which weighed 244 grams.

An experiment was made in A.D. 9 to circulate a new range of coins of no less than 28 denominations. These coins were made of gold, silver, tortoise-shell and cowries, as well as copper, and some of their shapes were modelled on the knives and spades that had circulated centuries previously. The experiment took place at a time of political disturbance, and neither the original set nor a simpler set which soon followed it met with popular acclaim or trust. With the restoration of stable government from A.D. 25, the five-*shu* piece again became the standard coin, and remained so for the rest of the Han period.

Official stipends were paid partly or wholly in coin; sometimes payment was made in the form of textiles, whose value was set out on a recognised scale of values. For example, we know of an officer serving at the north-west frontier, who received two rolls of silk, to the value of 900 coins, as his month's pay. With the breakdown of political stability and the loss of prosperity of the second century A.D. the use of coin tended to give place to a more general use of textiles or grain as a medium of exchange. Towards the end of the dynasty one writer at least was concerned with the effects of coin-hoarding and the tendency for coin to fly outwards from the centre. He raised the question of how circulation could best be stimulated, and whether the standard coin should be withdrawn and replaced by a lighter piece, weighing four *shu*; and evidently there were some who favoured the abolition of a system of coinage altogether.

Reference has already been made (p. 131) to Ch'ang-an's market-places and their supervision by officials. Such men may have been responsible for the collection of the tax that was levied on the day's transactions, and they may have had their quarters in the gateways that stood at the market's entrance. The markets were walled and closed to the public at nightfall; and the shops or stalls were laid out in rows together, with traders in the same commodity bidding against each other for custom.

Retail traders made their living by selling animals, raw materials, foodstuffs and manufactured goods. Horses and cattle, sheep and swine changed hands in the markets, and some businessmen dealt in slaves. There were specialists in horn, cinnabar, lacquer and raw sheep-skins. There were butcher's shops and cooked-meat stalls, as well as purveyors of syrup, pickled goods, dried fish, relishes, grains and fruit. Hardware stores sold utensils and equipment made of brass, iron or wood; carriage makers proudly displayed their light two-wheeled vehicles and their heavier ox-carts. Drapers stocked fine silken rolls and coarser fabrics of hemp, as well as made-up furs and furnishings such as mats or felts.

Although the histories sometimes include a record of the price at which grain sold in a particular year, such information is usually given to illustrate the abnormal conditions of famine or glut, and the figures can hardly be taken as representative.

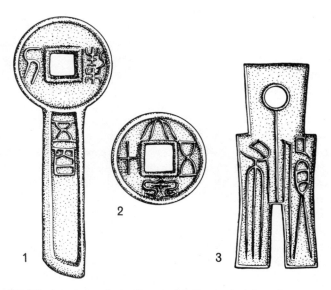

66 Three examples of a multi-denominational system, tried unsuccessfully for a while from A.D. 9. These coins were worth (1) 500, (2) 50 and (3) 25 single units

But some idea of the comparative values of commodities is afforded by a scheme that sets out over 30 different ways in which a businessman could earn a comfortable living that was comparable with that of a reasonably well-off marquis. Unfortunately the quantities that are involved cannot always be determined, and the scheme will not bear very close scrutiny; but it seems that an annual trade in any one of the following commodities would have produced the desired result:

head of horse	200
bamboo poles	10,000
jars of pickles and sauces	1000
rolls of variegated silk	1000
light carts	100
ox-carts	1000
brass utensils	30,000 *chin* [i.e. 7320 kilograms]
felts or mats	1000

From elsewhere, we learn that on one occasion in the north-west the sum of 40,000 coins would purchase two adult female slaves, 20 ox-carts or 10 farm-horses.

Fortunes could be made by iron-masters; by businessmen operating in several areas; or by the preparation and sale of salt. If a man could make a corner in scarce goods, such as grain in a time of famine, he could dispose of them very profitably. Money-lending is also listed among the ways of earning a comfortable income that are mentioned above, and an extreme case occurred in 154 B.C. when the government needed ready cash to put down a rebellion. A wealthy man who was willing to lend 1000 units of gold was evidently in a position to dictate his terms; and as the rebellion was repressed within three months, he was soon able to collect his interest which amounted to ten times the principal.

So from time to time the government took steps to divert such profits from the hands of the rich merchant, or to encourage him to undertake ventures that would benefit the community as well as his own pocket. Usually there were only small profits to be made by transporting grain, so the government had to reward a merchant for conveying a consignment over the long distances to the area where it was most needed. There were several schemes devised to stabilise prices or to bring about a regular and more beneficial means of transport; and in about 117 B.C. agencies were created to run the iron and salt mines as monopolies of the government, in place of the abandonment of these concerns to private enterprise (see Chapter 15).

Many a Han official would have affirmed in all sincerity that the resources of the empire were sufficiently large and varied to satisfy the population, and that there was no need to import goods from those unfortunate communities who lived beyond the limits of the emperor's authority. In practice, however, there was undoubtedly an exchange of Chinese goods, mainly silks, for luxury articles that the Chinese did not themselves produce, and it was in this way that governments could acquire a stock of horses or other animals. Other Chinese exports may have included iron and bronze manufactures, other than military weapons, and lacquer wares; and imports were by no means restricted to the necessities of life. Jade was brought in from Central Asia as a raw material on which

67 A market scene with the gate-way on the left. The figures in the storeyed building at the right probably represent an official talking to a tradesman, and the drum hanging in the upper part may have been used to signal the opening and closing hours of the market. Three transactions are in progress, and refreshments are being served

Chinese craftsmen could perform their miracles of delicate carving; and some of these pieces may have served as re-exports. Pearls were imported from the south; and while the imperial hunting parks were stocked with bizarre beasts such as lion or rhinoceros, other live imports included slaves or jugglers who may have learnt their skills by the shores of the Mediterranean sea.

We possess a few fragments of contracts or similar documents which regulated sales or loans between two Chinese parties to the transaction. These agreements specify the goods in question and their quantity (e.g., clothing, textile or land) together with the names of the parties and the witnesses. There is usually a reference to the agreed price and the date for completing the settlement. Servicemen who entered into dispute with each other in such transactions could refer the matter to their officers for arbitration.

Reference has been made above (p. 71) to the difficulties of transporting grain to the capital city and the assignment of servicemen both to this task and to the work of building roads or digging canals. For although there are several broad and lengthy rivers which traverse China from west to east, these do not form a fully adequate natural means of communication. In its lower reaches the Yellow River is liable to flood and to break its banks, and boatmen could not rely on finding a permanent course which would survive the river's meanderings. Further west, passage was seriously hampered by the cluster of rocks lying midstream, at a site which is now termed the San-men, or Gorge of the Three Gates. Moreover, the Yellow River itself did not lead directly to Ch'ang-an, which was reached by one of its tributary streams. This was the river Wei, whose twists and turns added considerably to the time needed for transport. As a result, the transport of grain from east China to the less productive metropolitan area was often slow and inefficient.

By the end of the sixth century A.D. a growing dependence on the grain grown in the Lower Yangtze Valley had resulted in the connection of several canals to form a system that would bring the grain-boats to the north-west from just that area. But for the Han period a further weakness in natural communications lay in the absence of a usable link between the north-west

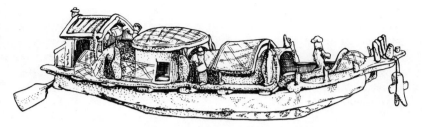

68 A river boat with living quarters.
From a clay model found in southern China

and the highly fertile reaches of the Upper Yangtze, i.e. the modern province of Ssu-ch'uan. The intervening territory is mountainous and wooded, and it proved impossible to make use of the small streams that fed the Wei and the Han rivers, as a means of joining the two areas. It may be noted that this problem has only been solved recently, thanks to the railway engineers of the twentieth century and their techniques.

Canals had been built in China from the fifth century B.C. at least. They were mostly designed to connect the smaller cities or states of the Huai River Valley, but perhaps the most famous artificial waterway of early times was the canal built to link the Yangtze and the Huai rivers for military purposes, in 487 B.C. The methods and speed of canal building must have improved considerably during the following centuries, with the more general use of iron and the growing ability of civil authorities to conscript and control larger forces of man-power. In the Han period canals were built for various purposes. There were attempts to solve the problem of the Yellow River by ensuring that the heavy weight of silt and water that had arrived from the Central Asian hills could find a passage to the sea. Such schemes depended on the combination of natural courses and artificial channels, or alternatively dykes, which would direct the flow to a safe outlet.

Nearer the capital city there were schemes to provide better transport and irrigation simultaneously by cutting channels which would connect two rivers. In 129 B.C. a project was put in hand to build a waterway that would link Ch'ang-an directly with the Yellow River. This was to take the place of the Wei River, and it was hoped that the distance would be reduced by two-thirds and the time needed for the transport of grain by a half. At the same time the population would benefit from the new supplies of water that they could draw for their fields. Conscript labour was put to the work which was finished in three years.

There are many other examples of the attention paid by Han governments to waterways. Some schemes were intended for military purposes in campaigns that were fought in the south. Clay models buried in tombs show us the sort of river boat used in those regions, and there are references to the 'tiered vessels' used for military purposes. Occasionally troops were carried by sea to extend Han dominion, in the south for instance or in Korea. Merchants' vessels may have been pioneering in Malayan waters, and when typhoons allowed, China's eastern coast may have seen peaceful traders as well as some pirates at work.

Travellers by land could use several types of road. Officials might ride on the imperial highways, provided that they did not infringe the central lane which was specially levelled and reserved for majesty. Some roads had been laid out for the

69 A light carriage with canopy; the driver sits on the right, the passenger on the left

70 A covered goods waggon. (The lines of the wheel and
roof appear thus on the original relief.)

movement of troops or supplies; but most frequent of all were
the rough and ready by-ways that led across the countryside;
and in mountainous areas travellers might pick their way along
the narrow tracks that local authorities had built and that stood
precariously on the hillside. There are several references to the
difficulties of constructing roads in these remote districts. We are
told that labourers were needed by the ten thousand, and that
their supplies had to be carried on their own backs.

Much of China's produce was conveyed from the fields to the
waterways or granaries in the humble ox-cart, and asses may
sometimes have been used to pull a waggon. But for the poorer
farmers, man-power took the place of draught-animals. In
mountainous regions mules were used as carriers and camels
were of obvious value on the routes that led out from Ch'ang-an
to the sands of the north-west. Horses were used more as a
luxury or for special purposes than for everyday transport, and
were on the whole restricted to officials and a few rich men.
There was a system of posts and horses kept by the government,
so that officials could travel at speed when this was necessary;
and this express service proved its worth in times of emergency.
Some individuals were perhaps able to maintain a similar
service for their own use. From time to time on their journeys
travellers would come up to a point of control, where it was
necessary to prove one's identity and satisfy the inspectors that
neither contraband goods nor persons required for arrest lay
concealed among the baggage.

71 This system of breast-strap harness was in regular use during the Han period, and provided a more efficient use of horse-power than earlier types

We can distinguish between various types of vehicle. For pomp or pleasure, there were first the luxuriously furnished coaches prepared for the emperor's own use. We have heard above (p. 140) of the posh cabs kept in Ch'ang-an's fashionable quarters, and we know of a few examples of show-cars, which carried a group of performing musicians or actors around town. The light carriages used by officials consisted of rectangular box-like structures borne on two wheels and pulled by a single horse between two shafts; and there was a central canopy which protected the great man from the heat of the day. Some of these carriages took a lictor with his axe on his way to his duties; and in other cases officials were accompanied by servants or runners. There were goods carts in which a farmer took his produce to market or to the official granary; these were fitted with sturdy wheels and all-round protection against the elements. There is a hint that these carts were constructed to carry a standard load of 25 tubs of grain, each containing one standard measure (i.e. about 20 litres). When two animals were yoked to a vehicle they usually rode abreast, but a tandem arrangement for four-wheeled carts was not unknown. For all cases the Han Chinese had devised an efficient means of harnessing the animals, so that they could exert the highest degree of tractive power without impeding their breathing.

A further means of transport, that was certainly used in the second century A.D. and probably before then, is seen in the single-wheeled barrow on which a man loaded his wares and which he pushed by hand. At a pinch these humble carriers could support the weight of a passenger; and shortly after the Han period they were used by a famous and ingenious military commander to supply his troops in a remote and inaccessible area.

13

The countryman and
his work

'The world is based on agriculture.' So runs the opening assertion of several edicts promulgated in the name of the Han emperors, and its repetition reveals an underlying characteristic of Chinese society that had been recognised by political theorists and statesmen early in the Han period. Agriculture was a mark of distinction between the Chinese and the alien; between the families which led a settled form of life under the protection of the emperor's government, and the nomad peoples, forced to seek their living from one pasture ground to the next, and unable to develop a stable form of society or an acknowledged form of political leadership.

A determination to extract the richest possible harvest from the soil had long moulded the social forms of the Chinese people; the force of family solidarity had been stressed by the need to devote maximum attention to the soil from all its members; imperial government and its system of revenues had been based on the assumption of a prosperous use of the land; and, as we have noticed (p. 152), there had arisen among some thinkers a feeling of distaste or protest against occupations of a less important nature. The Chinese knew only too well what results could ensue from nature's catastrophic interference with the work of the fields, from poor husbandry or lazy attention to the crops. And it was in the interests of all elements of society to ensure that the fruits of the earth were duly nurtured and gathered.

We can probably assume that the greater part of the registered population of Han China consisted of small households, each of four or five members who were actively engaged in working the land. From the point of view of the tax-gatherer these households were the individual units of the population whose occupations and movements could be partly controlled, and whose produce formed the basic revenues of state. But there were reasons why the Chinese would sometimes think in terms of cooperative units of several households. Chinese tradition had it that in the remote and glorious past a happy and peaceful way of life had rested on the productive work of eight house-holds who worked on adjoining plots of land, providing a sufficiency both for themselves and for the superior households of the nobility, whose hands were not soiled by field-work; and although it is more than questionable whether, or to what extent, such a cooperative scheme had ever been practised, the idea was by no means excluded from the minds of Han statesmen.

In any event the different types of land-tenure by non-working landlords, tenant-farmers or owner-farmers forced different parts of the community to take note of one another's existence during the course of the agricultural year. Moreover, there were other reasons provided by nature why small families could not hope to live an independent life on their own farms. The likelihood of drought or flood might persuade several households to work together to devise effective irrigation, or to build dykes to control or preserve the waters; or difficult com-

72 A rural scene in west China showing bird hunting and a river with water lilies and fish

73 Two reapers are cutting grain with scythes, and supplies are being brought to the men in the fields

munications from one village to another or to the nearest town could obviously be eased by corporate working. There were also occasions when the hand of government played a part in promoting agricultural production, for example in distributing seed or tools in time of distress; and it was to the granaries of the government that much of the corn found its way during a bumper season, if it was not to be allowed to run to waste.

Social stability and agricultural prosperity depended both on the will of government and on the forces of nature. A government's strength derived in the last resort from the extent of its revenue; and if maximum use was to be made of the soil and the available man-power, the government must refrain from taking the peasantry off the land to serve in campaigns, which would themselves require supplies from the home provinces. Similarly, if the hand of government was unduly harsh or grasping, the peasantry would be tempted to flee; and the fields would lie fallow. The numbers of such displaced persons who wandered around seeking a living by beggary or other means was increased considerably at times of natural disaster, when a village lay inundated and its inhabitants had taken to the hills; or when the survivors of drought had managed to escape from their parched fields to hunt for a livelihood elsewhere.

Once the peasantry had been uprooted, whether in the face of excessively harsh government or in retreat before the forces of nature, the power of the temporal government was already on the wane. Its revenues were declining, and its officials were losing their powers of coercion; and communities would grow up in the countryside which looked to other means of leadership. Displaced families could best find a living in the estates of the great land-owners, whose wealth and status ensured some degree of independence of civil government. In these large estates the displaced families would be given the seed, tools and draught-animals which they could not afford for their own plots; and they were also protected from official demands. As the power of government weakened, so did that of the large estate owners grow, thriving on the work of tenant or wage-earning peasantry, and on the armed men who were maintained as their protectors. By the second century A.D. the working conditions of the countryside were characterised as much by the dominance of the large families as they had been in earlier decades by the presence of the official. Some of the main economic advances of agricultural China (e.g., the development of mills and irrigational methods) may have originated in experiments that were made in these estates, or in the Buddhist communities which arose between the third and sixth centuries.

We shall never know what proportion of the sixty million registered inhabitants of A.D. 1–2 were actively engaged in growing cereal crops; and although the count of the population is accompanied by a figure for the extent of registered land that was then under the plough, there are too many unknown factors to make it possible to estimate for certain the extent of arable land per head of the population or its annual yield. But there are some indications which justify tentative conclusions.

The standard unit of measurement for land was the *mou*. Theoretically this consisted of a long strip measuring one by 240 paces (with each pace measuring six Han feet, or 140 centimetres), and the *mou* was thus equivalent to 0·1139 English acre. In practice fields were laid out in a variety of shapes, but

74 A relief from eastern China showing a hunting scene

75 A reconstruction of an agricultural technique evolved by Chao Kuo. According to the written description, there were six alternate furrows and ridges, each one foot wide and theoretically extending for 240 feet

surveys were made in terms of *mou*. Very tentatively we may assume that an average distribution would have amounted to perhaps 14 *mou* per head of the registered population, while remembering that no such distribution ever existed in fact. With the same reserve about an 'average' figure, we may think in terms of an annual output of cereal crops of 1·5 to 3 *shih* (with the *shih* being equivalent to almost 20 litres) per *mou*. We may also note, in passing, that the annual grain rations which were allowed from official stores on the north-west frontier varied from 14 to 43 *shih* according to the recipient's age and sex and the type of grain.

While rice has formed the staple cereal of southern China (i.e. from the Yangtze Valley and beyond), the northern provinces have lived off a diet of wheat or millet, and in the extreme north-west barley was probably one of the usual crops. The Han farmers grew a variety of grains, dependent on climate and soil; and these were used both as a solid food and for distilling liquor. The farmer's year was spent mainly in the repetitive and never-ending tasks of ploughing, sowing, hoeing and watering; and many a weary and anxious month passed before the peasant and his wife would know how abundant the harvest would be, always provided that it survived the natural hazards of the last, all important weeks before the gathering.

A number of technical improvements in the utilisation of land can be dated from the Han period; and despite the somewhat slow, if steady, pace at which innovations spread in the provinces there can be little doubt of their effect. The motive for the improvement of output can be traced easily enough to the need to feed the greater numbers who lived in the north-west, particularly in Ch'ang-an itself.

Before the Han period a somewhat rudimentary and

76 A ploughman with two oxen and an attendant. From a tomb built in A.D. 103

extravagant system of field-rotation may have been practised. Sometimes the land was worked in alternate years, or for one year in three, and at other times lay fallow to regain its strength. And before the Han period we hear of no systematic means of regulating the level of the soil in the fields, so as to direct the water where it was most needed and to concentrate the manures where they could be most effective. Improvements in these respects that were made from about 100 B.C. are ascribed to Chao Kuo, a skilled agriculturalist who had occasion to present his considered views to the government of the day. He advised that at the start of the farming year the six-foot-wide *mou* should be split into three shallow furrows, separated from each other by three raised ridges; furrow and ridge were each to measure one foot in width, and each year their relative positions were to be changed.

This change was brought about naturally as a result of the method of cultivation that Chao Kuo recommended. Previously, seed had been scattered, almost in broadcast fashion, on to the comparatively broad six-foot-wide *mou*, and labourers achieved this result by working upwards, from the low surrounding trenches where they stood. Under Chao Kuo's scheme, the seed was cast in regular lines along the furrows, and the men were able to concentrate it here far more easily, as they stood on the ridges and worked downwards into the furrows.

The change was simple, but its effects were potentially dynamic. The annual yield could now be the same from one year to the next, while a system of alternating the positions of the furrows and ridges took place almost spontaneously. For once the new shoots began to sprout, the weeds were removed from the raised ridges that separated the furrows. In the process, the soil was loosened and dropped into the furrows, where it would support the newly rising stalks. As the plants grew firmer, so was the process continued, until at the height of summer the ridges had been completely flattened out, and the new crop was embedded firmly enough to withstand wind and drought. Successful experiments in these methods were carried out in the metropolitan area in an attempt to put virgin ground under the plough. Production compared favourably with that of other fields, where the new methods had not been used; and they were soon applied in the far north-west, as a means of helping to supply the garrison forces.

The use of a new type of plough, equipped with a pair of ploughshares, possibly developed at this time. Chao Kuo is said to have favoured this implement, which was pulled by two oxen, with one man leading the way and two men controlling the handles (alternatively, there were two men controlling the animals, and the third took his station at the handles). As cattle were not always available, Chao Kuo soon had the peasantry shown how the ploughs could be pulled by man-power alone. A further technical innovation, possibly of the Han period, was a circular device which regulated the fall of the seed along the furrows.

The new plough did not come into general use immediately, nor did it render the old hand-worked appliances altogether obsolete; and although iron tools were perhaps being distri-buted at this time by the state agencies (see p. 189), the old-fashioned bifur-cated cultivator, of wood, was still in use in the second century A.D. More-over, there were several re-corded occasions of cattle plague during the Eastern Han period, and at such times the farmers may have reverted to the earlier models. In addition, a new scheme of land utilisation, which was evolved in about 20 B.C., was well suited to their use.

77 A shepherd with sheep. From a tomb built in A.D. 103

This scheme is described in a book that has mostly disappeared; as in Chao Kuo's method, the principal object was to concentrate effort and resources where they were most needed, and to make use of unexploited soil. The plan provided for a more intensive and economic use of water and manure which included animal products and crushed bones, so that the young shoots would derive maximum benefit. Foot-wide and foot-deep channels were to be dug at suitable intervals across the fields. Grain-shoots were then planted in double rows along the channels, lying half a foot away from each other and a quarter of a foot from the sides of the channels; and a thin covering of soil was added on top. For this sort of working, which was suited to areas where ploughing space was restricted, the small hand-digger was of more practical use than the ox-drawn plough.

The farmers' main occupation lay in the production of life's necessities, i.e. grain for food, and hemp for the coarse raiment in which most of the population were clothed. But where land and climate permitted, the countryman could raise reasonably high profits by other undertakings; by stock-breeding or pasturing horses or cattle, sheep or pigs; by keeping fish-farms or maintaining timber-woods and bamboo-groves. Fruit-growing was practised in both the north and the south, as and where conditions favoured chestnut, date or citrus fruit. Some countrymen made a living from mulberry orchards and the product of the silk-worm, or from the lac tree whose lacquer was used so lavishly for decorative purposes by the wealthy; and market-gardeners who lived near the cities could ply a trade in vegetables or seasonings such as leeks or ginger. As yet there was no widespread growth of tea, cotton or sugar. The tea-bush was doubtless known in some parts of the south, but the drink did not yet feature as a daily or common beverage. Knowledge of the grape had been brought from the trade-routes that led to Central Asia, and vineyards were kept for the use of the Palace. The spirits that were distilled somewhat extravagantly from grain made their appearance at religious functions and occasions of merry-making, and supplies were sometimes distributed by imperial bounty. Cane-sugar was probably grown in the south but some centuries had to pass before its distribution became general. Sheep were kept for

78 Pigsty, with stairway to upper chamber used as a lavatory

79 Sheep's pen, with child rider: model in red pottery from a tomb

mutton or for their fleeces which could be shaped into warm garments; but the Han Chinese were not accustomed to process sheep's wool into textiles, as were their neighbours in Central Asia.

The surviving fragments of the textbook on agricultural methods of about 20 B.C. which is quoted above (see p. 170) include the following advice and directions for growing gourds:

Plough ten *mou* of good-quality land in the third month, and form into foot-square pits, each one foot deep. These should be pounded hard with a rammer, so that they will retain water. The pits should be separated from each other by one pace [six Han feet*]. Sow with four seeds each, and pack with one *tou** of silk-worm lime mixed with loam. Sprinkle with two *sheng** of water, and, if in dry ground, repeat. When three fruit have set on each plant, beat with a horse-whip to prevent straggling growth; and note that the more fruit that grow, the smaller each one will be. Straw should be placed below the fruit to prevent them coming into contact with the soil and getting scabbed. Select the fruit most suitable for calabashes, and rub with the hand from calyx to base so as to remove the down. This will prevent the fruit growing too long and will allow thickening. Gather the fruit in the eighth month [i.e. from mid-September] after the first light frosts.

A ten-foot deep pit should be dug and lined with straw to a thickness of one foot on each side. The fruit should be laid here in rows in their natural positions, and each layer of gourds should be covered with two feet of soil. The fruit should be taken out after twenty days, and it will be found that they are golden and of fine quality, ready for splitting into calabashes. The white flesh below the skin may be used as pig food and is very rich. The seeds may be burnt for purposes of lighting, and will be found to shed a brilliant light.

If each plant bears three gourds, there will be 12 to each pit, and the produce of one *mou* of land will be 2880 fruit, giving a total of 57,600 calabashes from ten *mou*. These may be priced at ten cash each, so that the total value of the crop will be 576,000 cash. For production costs, allow 26,000 cash, to cover 200 *shih* of silk-worm lime and expenses for ox-plough and labour. There remains a profit of 550,000 cash, together with pig-food and fuel for lighting.

* The Han foot measures 23 cm. Equivalents for units of volume were: 1 *shih* = 19·9 litres; 1 *tou* = 1·9 litres; 1 *sheng* = 199 ccm.

A number of mechanical contrivances had been devised to aid the Han farmer in his work. Long hammers were laid out horizontally, with the central point resting on a fulcrum where it could pivot; and at the end opposite the head, a man would stand on pedals, speeding the machine into action. There must have been several uses for these hammers other than beating the husks off grain (e.g., pounding earth, in the processes of building); and there is some evidence to suggest that Han engineers had succeeded in harnessing animal-power and water-power to operate these hammers mechanically. Fans were used to separate the chaff from the kernels of the grain. These were fitted to containers into which the grain was fed, and a crank handle was sometimes used to turn the wheel. The final reduction of grain to flour was done first by means of pestles and mortars, some of which were made in bronze; but there were also handmills worked with a circular movement, and probably made of wood, baked clay or stone. It is also possible that towards the end of the Han period milling was done by means of a cylindrical roller drawn evenly across the grain.

Perhaps the most arduous, necessary and continuous task that faced the farmer was that of lifting water from the wells or irrigation channels to maintain a steady and constant supply

80 Grain milling: two men work pedal-operated hammers while on the right a load is being emptied for sifting. In the background there is a raised granary

81 Clay model of a wooden well-head, with a pulley and simulated mortice and tenon joints for fitting the component wooden parts together. From a tomb probably dated A.D. 170–180

to the fields. One of the simplest aids took the form of a pole suspended horizontally, to swing over a central vertical support. A bucket was attached to the end that lay immediately over the water, and was lowered for filling; and to raise the load the peasant simply fitted a counter-weight at the opposite end of the pole, thus lifting the bucket to the required level. From models that were buried in tombs we know that some wells were fitted with a protective housing and roof, and that a pulley was built-in, so that buckets could be raised or lowered by rope.

The elevation of water from irrigation channels that lay below the level of the fields was probably done by human foot-power. By revolving a horizontal shaft to which an endless chain had been fitted, it was possible to depress a series of empty compartments or containers into the stream and bring them back filled, so that their contents could be delivered into the fields. At a later period this type of pumping device was operated by water-power or animal-power; and it has by no means been abandoned in the face of the more modern techniques of the twentieth century.

We possess no detailed contemporary record of the Han countryman's year whose value can compare with that of the manorial records or illuminated manuscripts which bear witness to the life of the farmer in mediaeval Europe. But fragments of a short text on husbandry that is ascribed to Ts'ui Shih (c. 100–170) set out an ideal and doubtless stylised programme of the different occupations of the farmer and his household for the 12 months of the year. Although the author's family came from the north-east (near the modern Peking), the text was probably written with the conditions of Lo-yang in mind.

The Ts'ui family had been land-owners, but by the second century A.D. their fortunes were not what they had been. Indeed, the expenses incurred in providing his father with a suitable funeral and in having a proper set of monuments erected left Ts'ui Shih in a state of penury, and he was forced at one time to earn a living in the much despised liquor trade. At a later stage in his life, when he went to serve as a provincial governor in the north, Ts'ui Shih came face to face with the conditions of poverty from the other side of the fence. The district was well-suited to the growth of hemp, but the new governor was shocked to find that the inhabitants used grasses as a protection against the cold and that textile-weaving was hardly known. Ts'ui Shih soon saw to it that the necessary equipment and instruction was provided so that locally woven textiles could be worn.

His set of rules for husbandry are concerned with a variety of subjects, which range from religious festivals and education to domestic economy and the preparation of remedies for sickness. The farmer is told when he should plant, weed and harvest his various crops; and his womenfolk when they should set in motion the different processes of silk-production, weaving, dyeing and tailoring. There is a set programme for processing foods, gathering wild plants and distilling their drugs for medicines; and for the maintenance of property and the care of domestic and farming equipment. The head of the family is advised when he should send his youngsters off to school, and at what times of the year it is favourable to buy in the stores that he needs, or to sell his own produce.

The book starts with instructions for keeping the festival of the New Year's Day, on the first day of the first month.* The whole family must purify themselves before the offerings of strong drink may be presented at the shrine; and once this part of the ceremony was over, all members, senior and junior

---

* These months are those of the luni-solar calendar (see pp. 103f.), and corresponded very roughly as follows: first month, from mid-February; third month, from mid-April; sixth month, from mid-July; ninth month, from mid-October.

82 Training a horse with a rope, and an unidentified
object on the left

alike, should gather in their appointed places of precedence to
sit in attendance before their ancestors. Women and children,
sons and grandsons duly presented themselves to the head of the
family and raised their goblets in due solemnity. For this was
one of the principal occasions of the year for the family to pray
for happiness and prosperity; and a day could be suitably
chosen to hold the ceremony of giving a youth his cap, as a
means of showing his acceptance as an adult member of the
community.

The first month was a season when the agricultural year had
hardly begun, and the opportunity could be taken to send boys
to school. But there were trees which could be transplanted,
such as bamboo, pine or oak, or those that produced lacquer or
oils; and a man could safely sow melons and gourds, onions and
garlic. The decayed leaves should be swept up and the fields
manured. Trees could be pruned, but bamboo and timber
should not be felled.

There were other religious occasions during the year. In the
second and eighth months offerings of leeks and eggs were
presented to the lord of the soil and the spirits of the seasons;
in the eighth month millet and piglets were to be reverently
presented to the ancestral graves; and a whole host of rites
which were to be performed in the twelfth month in honour of
spirits and ancestors included the slaughter of pigs and sheep,
fasting and purification, and offerings of wine. There were also
the festivals that accompanied climatic changes such as the
summer and winter solstices, as well as the spring festival of
re-awakening. The first and twelfth months were the correct
time for paying dutiful visits to one's social superiors; the second

83 Clay model of a round granary, from southern China

and third for a man to practise his archery, so that he would be ready to deal with robbers; and at the same time a man should repair his gates and doors for the protection of his household. In the ninth month a wise man would check the state of his weapons; and he should also spare a thought for the orphans, widows and sick members of the clan, and provide for their needs in the coming winter.

Heavy ground was broken up in the first month; good arable in the second; and light sandy soils in the third; and in some of the fields this work might continue right through to the seventh month. Hay was cut in the fifth and eighth months, and the sixth month was the time for hoeing. For the first eight months of the year there was usually some crop or vegetable to be sown; in addition to cereals there were gourds, beans or hemp, and the right time depended on seasonal conditions, such as the rains of the third month or the summer solstice of the fifth month. There were a number of herbs to be collected and drugs to be compounded in the fifth month, when it was advisable to take certain hygienic precautions. For the *Yin* and the *Yang* were locked in combat, and it would be wise for man and wife to sleep in separate rooms.

Meanwhile the women of the household were busy nurturing their silk-worms and keeping careful watch over their life-cycle so that the threads could be used to best advantage. In the sixth month they would be spinning the textiles, before settling down to the summer tasks of washing old clothes, cutting new clothes and dyeing the silk cloth. In the tenth month they were best employed on working hemp and fashioning sandals; and there were few months in the year when the country household was not engaged in brewing liquors or preserving foods with the help of seasonings that had been gathered from the woods at the right time.

Spring was a time for re-plastering the walls of the house and applying a fresh coat of lacquer where this was suitable. In the

178

fifth month a farmer should remember that the seasonal rains would soon turn the lanes into an impassable quagmire, and it would be prudent to lay in a supply of food and firewood. It was also a time to buy a supply of wheat-bran, which should be dried and stored in jars. These needed to be sealed carefully so that they did not breed maggots; and come the winter the supply could be used as fodder for the horses. Granaries and storage pits should be repaired in the ninth month; and at the end of the year the far-sighted farmer would assemble his plough for the coming year's work and take care to feed his oxen to their fill, so that they would be fit and strong to face the labour of the working year that lay ahead.

14

Craftsmanship

Chinese textiles in use during the Han period were woven from hemp, or other vegetable fibres or silk; and although the greater part of the population were probably dressed in coarse hempen garments, it is of silk fabrics that most is known and of which we can speak here. For, scanty though they are, the surviving fragments of Han silks are more extensive than those of other materials. In addition, the manufacture of silk cloth has always occupied a high place in the priorities of China's products. It has been associated with imperial patronage and has served to supply the official with his robes; and it is likely that in this respect as elsewhere elements of Han practice tended to form the standard norm of Chinese usage.

There was a long tradition of sericulture in China, extending back to at least 1500 B.C.; and by the time of the Han empire, silk-farmers must have acquired considerable skill in the delicate task of nurturing the worms to best advantage. Cultivated silk is made by reeling the very long (several hundred metres) filaments from the cocoons in continuous lengths; and this result can only be achieved by keeping a rigorous watch over the life-cycle of the worms, ensuring that the same stage of development has been reached simultaneously, and reeling the silk before it is spoiled or broken by natural processes.

No remains survive of the devices on which the Han Chinese wove their plain or patterned silks, but from a consideration of the extant fragments of materials and two rather rough illustrations it is possible to infer something about the looms that were in use. The great advantage of silk over vegetable fibres lies in the length of the natural thread, which can be used directly to form the warp of the material (i.e. it forms the longitudinal threads running along the length of the bale; the weft threads form the shorter cross-threads that run from side to side). The finished fabric is stronger and can be stretched for greater lengths than materials made of other fibres; and of all fabrics it is the most comfortable to wear and the most beautiful to behold.

It is likely that the Han textile experts used a loom that was set horizontally, with the warp threads stretched out along the length. Weft threads were inserted from side to side alternately over one and under the next warp; and to achieve the alternation needed to produce the intricate patterns that were in use a form of heddle may have been operated by foot. Vague as the details of these devices must remain, it seems that the Han machinery, or some parts of it, can be classed in general terms with the draw-looms used in the western world from the sixth century A.D.

The available specimens of Han textiles derive almost exclusively from the north-western parts of the empire. Pieces of cloth or garment have been found in the remains of those very same watchtowers and fortresses which have yielded fragments of written records compiled between about 100 B.C. and A.D. 100; and other examples have been found in sites lying further west, on the communications' route that the travellers took into Central Asia. The sites have provided very few examples of complete garments. Manufactured silk was expensive, and it is likely that clothes were worn until the last possible moment before being discarded as useless, and that some of the tailor's skill was devoted to making patchwork clothes from the small squares of material that could be salvaged. Surviving remnants have been identified as parts of collars and sleeves, bows, sashes, and footwear, and only two complete pieces have been identified for certain. These comprise a woman's hood, made of two pieces of red silk and fastened at the collar by means of a silken cord; and a needle case made up of pieces of five different coloured silks, including wine-red, deep blue and several shades of blue and green. The case measured 10·5 by 8 centimetres, and retains two iron needles that had presumably been plied at Edsen-gol.

More durable clothes were worn by the servicemen who formed the garrison there. The outer layer of their garments was made of a good-quality single-coloured silk, and the linings were of a firm material of natural colour. Between the two silk layers fabrics of vegetable fibre were used to add body and weight, and in some cases silk-wadding was used as a means of padding. There were many forms of stitching used to sew patches together and for seams, and clothes were fastened together either with loops and buttons or by two bands that were tied together.

The dimensions of silk bales can be calculated both from some of the surviving pieces and from the lucky find of an abandoned roll, left by the way on the 'Silk Road' of Central Asia. Undyed materials were made up with a selvage on each side in widths of between 45 and 50 centimetres (i.e. 2 and 2·2 Han feet). An inscription on one piece that had probably been manufactured in east China (modern Shantung) for the export market in about A.D. 90 gives the following specification: width 2·2 feet; length 40 feet; weight 25 *liang*; value 618 coins (i.e. width 50 centimetres; length 9·2 metres; weight 380 grams). The monetary value of the roll can be compared with the monthly stipends of officers serving in the north-west, at rates which were fixed between 360 and 3000 coins; and we know of at least one case in which an officer who was entitled to a monthly stipend of 900 coins was actually paid in two rolls of silk.

The density of the weaves varies considerably, from 16–20 threads per centimetre at the lowest to 140–200 at the highest; and there were different types of weave, such as taffeta, with as many weft threads as there were warps, and warp-rep, where the warp threads were twice as dense as those of the weft. There were also gauzes and crêpes, and a patterned material whose effect was similar to that of modern table-linen and which is usually described as 'damask'. There was presumably some relation between the quality of the material and its use, and we know of roughly fashioned red silk which was used as part of a man's coat, in contrast with the fine taffetas that were fashioned into a lady's festive dress. The rich vocabulary of contemporary Han texts testifies to the great variety of materials that were available for the rich, who could choose their dazzling whites, their many-coloured materials or cloth in which gold leaf or foil had been skilfully introduced. There were also local distinc-

84 A silver dress-hook with a circular button on the
reverse side beneath the central knob

tions, between the textiles of the east and the
west, and between different types of manufacture, such as those of the palace-workshops, of
home-industry or of the professional producers.

Silks were sometimes used together with
materials made of vegetable fibres. Cotton had
not yet been introduced to Chinese use, and
the normal substances were hemp and a type
of nettle. Nettle-cloth was considerably softer
and warmer than that made of hemp, and could
resemble modern linens and be used for underwear. The Chinese themselves did not develop
the use of wool fabrics as a native undertaking,
but we hear of finely spun grass-cloth from the
west, and multi-strand weaves from the south.
There is an interesting example of the combined
use of silk and vegetable fibres in a shoe woven
for a young woman, of which the sole is now
missing. This measures 23 centimetres in length, and was made
of multi-coloured material. That part of the upper which
covered the toes incorporated two bands of decoration, and the
complete shoe had probably included a lining made of silk.

These fabrics were made up in single colours such as brown,
blue, green or red, while yellow was perhaps reserved for
imperial use alone. But the most exquisite and expensive of all
materials was the famous 'ice-white' brand, with its brilliant
lustre, whose delicate and fine glory could not withstand ex-
posure to sun or rain. There were also silks woven with as many
as five different colours.

A number of elements can be discerned in the stylistic and
decorative motifs of Han textiles. Some patterns consisted
entirely of geometric shapes, such as checks or diamonds
repeated endlessly; and from these there developed the use of
zig-zag bands, themselves lozenge-shaped, which served to
separate the units of a major design into smaller compartments.
Or else, this division was effected by curvilinear patterns, sometimes described as 'cloud-scroll'. Encompassed by these dividing

lines or bands we find animals such as the dragon or phoenix depicted in the stylised or conventional forms that their symbolic significance demanded. Sometimes there are pairs of dragons or horses confronting each other, and at least one of the surviving damasks carries a row of fish in its design.

The characteristic shape of the Han coin—a circle enclosing a small square—appears on one fragment of material, and it is open to question whether this was intended as a symbol of wealth or of the circular universe embracing the square earth (see p. 118). A stylised series of closely grouped parallel lines that appears as part of a system of separating birds or other figures from each other is possibly to be explained as a symbolic means of effecting a transfer from one world to another; and just as the Han smiths who fashioned bronze mirrors often incorporated a series of characters which bore a felicitous message, so too did the textile designers programme their looms to reproduce continuously prayers for 'ten thousand life-times, and all you wish' or 'many years and long life, with a goodly blessing of sons and grandsons'.

In addition to patterned fabrics, we possess four valuable fragments of embroidered material where a highly developed skill is exhibited. Silken thread was applied to fabrics by chain-stitching, and even in the few available specimens it is possible to see signs of personal motives that lay behind these artistic endeavours. The fragments include parts of ladies' bags,

85 A piece of silk patterned with designs in blue, black and white on a red background. Two of the four characters of a blessing are seen duplicated here

possibly made to contain mirrors. These are decorated with roundels or twirling patterns, inspired perhaps by the embroiderer's imagination, perhaps by the world of nature; and there is one sad example of Han symbolism in an eight-centimetre square of red rep, embroidered with blue, brown and yellow silks. This square lay on the breast of a young girl who was buried in full dress

86 Reconstruction of the single-piece formal robe for men and women

in the sands of Central Asia; and the design that was lovingly placed over her body incorporated stylised forms of the cicada, the symbol of re-awakening which a family may well have wished for the girl whose loss they mourned.

The main centres of textile production lay in east China, where both hemp and silk were made up in bales, and three official agencies which were responsible for preparing the imperial robes were situated in this area. There was also a secondary centre of production in the west, which was at first concerned with hemp only, and whose products were finding their way by devious paths to north India during the second half of the second century B.C.; and towards the end of the Han period western China had won a reputation for the gilded cloth that it was producing. We do not hear much of silk production south of the Yangtze River before the Eastern Han period. In some parts, this deficiency evidently made it difficult for the local inhabitants to obtain shoes or sandals, and in about A.D. 85 a regional inspector in the modern area of Hunan reported the shocked dismay with which he heard of the prevailing habit of walking barefoot. Despite references to the regulations for the forms of dress worn by the emperor and court on occasions of religious ceremony or audience, these cannot be reconstructed with accuracy, in the absence of material evidence or contemporary illustrations. For the men there seems to have been considerable emphasis on the type of headgear, while the women who attended some of these functions had to be content with ornaments rather than hats, and to make full use of decorative hair-pins, earrings or pendants. Fig. 86 shows an attempt to reconstruct the basic pattern of the robes cut for men and women to wear on formal occasions.

Servicemen were issued with tunic, trousers, socks and footwear, and, perhaps, underwear. There is, however, insufficient information to warrant a general statement or description of the working dress used by ordinary people.

Some of the finest surviving examples of the work of Han craftsmen and artists are seen in the lacquered boxes, bowls and other articles of daily use which have been found in a remarkably good state of preservation in a number of Han tombs. They have remained unblemished throughout 20 centuries thanks to the preservative quality of lacquer, i.e. the juice tapped from the lac trees that grew in western, north-western and probably eastern China. Once this juice has been refined and the excessive moisture eliminated it may be stored for application to wooden or textile substances; and provided that the application covers the complete surface, the article will survive immersion in water for, literally, centuries. In addition, the hard finish forms an excellent surface for the painter, who uses a brush and lacquer itself to form his designs; alternatively it is possible to engrave the hardened surface and to form a design either by carving or by inlay.

The durable qualities of lacquer work were well known to the Han craftsmen, who used the substance for practical as well as ornamental purposes. There were not only lacquered articles of daily use such as cups, plates and dishes, or ladies' toilet requisites; military equipment such as sword-sheaths or shields were coated with this preservative, as were many of the component parts of carriages; and coffins themselves, together with a whole variety of funerary equipment, were treated with the substance.

In addition to the private enterprise which was probably responsible for fashioning lacquer ware, there were at least three government-sponsored workshops in A.D. 1–2 which specialised in this work. Some of their products travelled widely, as can be seen from an example of a lacquered beaker found at a Han colonist's grave in Korea. The inscription on the beaker

gives the year of manu-
facture as corresponding
to A.D. 55, and the maker
is named as the Workshop
of Kuang-han (i.e. near
the modern Ch'eng-tu).
There were several grades
of product, ranging from
the simple wooden vessels,
which formed the majority
of the pieces, to the luxury
manufactures in which a
lacquer coating had been
applied to a hempen
textile; and there were
intermediate grades when
a wooden base was first

87 The decorative pattern (yellow
and pink on a black background)
of a lacquered bowl

padded with a textile and the coating then added on top.
Before the lacquer treatment, there was a priming coat, and
the lacquer itself was applied in several layers, of which the
final one demanded the highest skill, so as to produce the
smooth texture and even finish that was required. Inscriptions on articles name the craftsmen who had been responsible
for the various processes of priming, lacquering, gilding,
painting, engraving or polishing; and, as on the inscriptions
which are found on other products of the government's factories, the names of the officials who supervised the work are
usually appended.

At first, scarlet and black were used as the basic colours for
decoration, but before the end of the Han period lacquer goods
were being painted in green, yellow or blue, in gold or silver.
While a brush was used for free designing, the perfect accuracy
of some of the geometric patterns makes it likely that the
craftsmen may sometimes have used a mechanical device. The
surface could be ornamented not only by engraving characters
of Chinese writing or other designs, but also by the inlay of
precious and glittering materials such as gold, silver, bronze or
tortoise-shell.

The surviving examples of textiles and lacquer wares provide
an insight into the skilled work of Han craftsmen and the use

which they made of their opportunities to demonstrate their artistic leanings. It must, however, be realised that many of the more commonplace products were of a far lower standard than those illustrated or described here, and that the everyday life of the Han peasant relied on equipment of a far more humble standard. Much of the output of the Han textile mills or lacquer shops was of a cheaper quality than that described above. Similarly the work of the sculptors and painters who embellished the homes and tombs of the rich must be contrasted with the products of the craftsmen who worked as potters, or joiners, or in leather, and whose output of earthenware, wooden or bamboo goods provided the farming families with the rough and ready domestic equipment that they could afford.

15

Industry and
technology

The Han economy rested first and foremost on agricultural production, and the great majority of the inhabitants spent their working lives in these wearisome and sometimes unrewarding tasks. But with the passage of time the government began to spread its interests more widely and to promote other occupations that served the more sophisticated life of the palace and the more highly advanced technical standards of daily life. By about 100 B.C. the government had come to realise the importance of mineral products and the need to ensure that these were being exploited efficiently and distributed fairly. It had not passed unnoticed that immense fortunes had been amassed in the past by a few magnates who operated the salt or iron industries, and it was felt that these should be managed by official agencies to avoid the practice of private monopolies.

At the same time similar agencies were being established to superintend timber forests in the west and fruit orchards in the south. The palace itself was demanding a supply of luxuries and manufactures, with the result that special workshops or factories had been founded. These employed craftsmen who worked in metal and wood, artists who were skilled in paint and lacquer, and the hands who produced the delicate textiles that were suitable for the court's use. These developments met with some criticism, as they were thought to be diverting energy from the stern business of producing life's necessities. For example, we read of the strictures of Kung Yü in about 45 B.C., referring to the employment of several thousand men in each of the three textile agencies in east China, and to the vast

88   Iron-working: on the left two men operate bellows, from which a
tube passes, apparently underground, to the anvil, where men are
forging the metal

expenses of the official establishments responsible for metal-
lurgical work in the west.

Altogether 48 iron-agencies were established in A.D. 1–2.
They were all placed north of the Yangtze River, and the great
majority lay in the valleys of the Yellow or Huai rivers and in
the Shantung peninsula. Two or three were situated in the
north-east, towards Manchuria, and there were several in the
south-west near the modern town of Chungking. From traces of
over ten sites of iron-shops and their workings that have been
found recently, it is possible to learn something of the processes
that were involved in the industry, and the size of the installations at some of the larger sites lends some credence to Kung
Yü's statement that a force of over 100,000 men was employed
annually in the iron and copper mines.

At the sites of Han iron towns that were situated in the
modern province of Ho-nan there were pits, foundries and living
quarters, and samples of materials range from crude ore to
finished articles and some of the equipment used in the process.
At one site there were some 20 working locations, in addition to
storage pits, furnaces and cooling tanks. From these traces it
can be concluded that the ores were hammered and then sorted
by sieves into ingots of the same size, and proportionate quantities of chemicals were added at various stages of the process
so as to bring about the necessary fusion.

There are many examples of the farming tools turned out
by the foundries; of the shares that were fitted to the ox-drawn
ploughs; of the working heads fixed to wooden handles for the
peasant who was digging, hoeing or weeding; and, less frequently, of the seed-boxes that accompanied the ploughman.
Some of these tools were cast with a written character or two

to signify the agency where they had been made; and it is possible that the promotion of Chao Kuo's agricultural techniques (see pp. 167f.) was first undertaken in conjunction with the distribution of these tools from the government's workshops.

Iron weapons of war were produced in greater numbers during the Han period than previously, but there is no means of determining how far the factories could supply the needs of the forces. There were iron and bronze swords and spears, as well as helmets and defensive armour; and consignments of arrowheads were plentiful enough to enable some guardsmen at the front to carry an issue of 150 arrows. But although iron was taking a dominant place in the manufacture of these pieces of equipment, one of the most notable products of the Han metal worker was the bronze trigger fitted to the cross-bows. These instruments were made with a very considerable degree of precision, and comprised several component parts that were fitted together with the greatest accuracy. A catch, which held the bowstring, and a control lever which released the arrow were fitted by means of pins to a principal box-like part; and some triggers were equipped with a graduated sight, so that the aim could be adjusted to suit the distance of the target. Many of these triggers bear an inscription giving details of manufacture. Domestic utensils manufactured in iron have also been found in some of the tombs, and include lamps, cooking pots, cooking stoves and knives.

At one bronze foundry that was discovered recently the shafts were driven 100 metres deep. There are signs that the installation had included ladders and iron tools for working the mine, and that the passage-ways had been carefully laid out with timbers. Round ingots were turned out here, weighing between five and 15 kilograms and inscribed with the mark of the particular

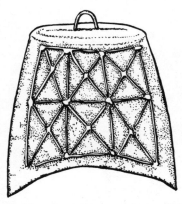

89 A bronze bell with formal pattern

workshop (e.g., East no. 60, or West no. 53). Another site produced rectangular ingots with a weight of 34 kilograms and a copper content of 99 per cent. These were inscribed with a note of the weight and a serial number.

While iron was taking the place of bronze for the manufacture of tools, bronze was used in the Han period for minting coin and casting mirrors. The five-*shu* piece (see pp. 153f.) was made with the use of moulds, of which a number have been found, and at least six sites of government mints have been identified near Ch'ang-an. Reference has been made above (p. 118) to the artists' use of bronze mirrors as a medium for the expression of highly decorative and symbolic designs. These were cast from clay moulds.

There are many other examples of pieces fashioned by the iron and bronze smiths for decorative or functional purposes, and in many cases an attempt was made to satisfy the demands of both the user and the viewer. There were bronze bells and vases; dishes and spoons; incense-burners; and personal ornaments to wear. When a ring was fixed to a building it was held by means of a bronze holder; and the government had standard weights and measures made in bronze for the verification of commercial practice. The inscriptions that appear on some of

90 A bronze container, for heating wine, dated 26 B.C. The lid has a ring and three fixed handles and there are two rings mounted on the side of the vessel. The animals on the decorative bands include the monkey, camel, ox, hare, sheep, deer, tiger and various birds

these pieces are sometimes highly informative, as they declare the capacity or weight of the object in Han measurements; very often the date of manufacture is given, with the names of the chief officials who had superintended production in the workshop or inspected the finished article and passed it as fit for distribution. There are also specimens of local iron and bronze products made in foundries that lay beyond the control of the Han official, outside the commanderies of the north-east or south-west.

91 Design engraved in the base of a bronze basin dated A.D. 129

The staple food of most Chinese consisted of cereals, and salt formed an essential adjunct if a proper dietary balance was to be maintained. There is reason to believe that this requirement was recognised and partly met by the commissariat of the Han forces, in view of the accounts that we possess of the distribution of a salt ration to the men. Supplies of salt, however, were limited to the products of a few localities, and the effective command of these resources could be operated as a highly profitable monopoly. Several cases had already been known at the time when the government decided to take over the industry into its own hands (about 117 B.C.).

The provisions made at that time resulted in the establishment of a number of agencies, which were mostly posted north of the Huai River. In A.D. 1–2 there was a total of 34 agencies, of which some dozen operated along the coast of the Shantung peninsula, drawing natural salt from the sea. Here the process of evaporation and purification was comparatively simple and probably depended on the use of a series of tanks or pans. But elsewhere, for example in sites that lay near Manchuria, the Ordos Desert or in Ssu-ch'uan, the rock-salt or brine lay at

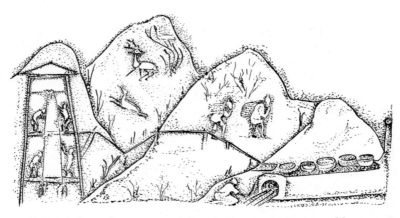

92 Salt-mining: four men with winding gear are working at a derrick to raise brine from the mine. A bamboo pipe-line conveys this for evaporation to the pans seen on the right above a furnace, which is possibly heated with natural gas. Two men are carrying loads of salt(?) away

considerable depths below the earth's surface and production demanded considerable engineering skill.

Salt-mining is depicted on several moulded bricks that have been found in Ssu-ch'uan. There were drills that may have penetrated over 600 metres into the earth; and the precious mineral deposits were brought to the surface by long tubular buckets that were probably made of locally grown bamboo. These were lowered by means of a winding gear and pulley; once the contents had been hauled to the surface it was conveyed on its next stage, presumably by bamboo pipe-line, if the practice of the twentieth century at the same sites can be taken as a guide. This led to suitably sheltered pans where the liquid could be dried out; and it is possible that the fires lighted below the pans were fed on natural gas, brought from the mine by the same means of conveyance.

The pretext for the debate on national policy which was staged in 81 B.C. (see pp. 137f.) was the need to reconsider the value of the state's monopoly of the salt and iron industries. A spokesman who argued the case for restoring these undertakings to private hands accused the iron-agencies of failing to provide the tools that the ordinary farmer needed; for they were obliged to spend their efforts in meeting the other demands that the government presented, for goods that were of less utilitarian value; and the shortage of the right sort of tools with a sharp cutting edge meant that the peasant had to work very hard for a meagre return. In defence of the monopolies it was claimed that only a centralised control of the mines and the iron industry could produce goods that were of a standard quality and price. But the critics had the last word. They referred to the reasonable price of salt and the fine quality of iron tools that had been available when it had been possible for any member of the public to take a lease on these undertakings; and these benefits were to be contrasted with the shoddy and expensive goods turned out by the unwilling labour of the agencies. Under a system of competition, eager hands had worked to turn out first-rate products, and people had been able to procure the articles they needed at reasonable prices. But under the public monopoly there was no choice of quality—all the goods were bad; and as the tools were so dear, the poorer farmers had to till the fields with wooden ploughs and weed the soil with their bare hands.

There were in addition eight government agencies which were responsible for various types of manufacture in different provinces, but their specialities cannot be completely identified. Two, that were established in the west, may have been concerned with fancy metal workings, such as decorative inlay work, or the production of the famous knives of Shu. The others were perhaps engaged in exploiting local materials.

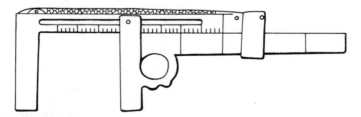

93 More refined than most other examples of simple foot-rules, this measuring instrument can be adjusted by means of a pin and slot to measure in tenths of an inch (·23 cm). An inscription on the other side gives the date of manufacture as a day corresponding to 15 January A.D. 9

Before picking up their hammers, saws or axes, or setting to work to drill, chisel or plane their wood, the Han carpenters must often have set their foot-rules to their material. These bronze bars were sometimes made with a covering arm which could be swung into position to protect the carefully marked surface. Usually these were graduated in divisions of the ten inches of the foot (i.e. 23 centimetres), and each inch was further subdivided into tenths. A remarkable example of a rather shorter ruler, which measured six inches only, bears a dated inscription of A.D. 9. This tool was made to enable a craftsman to retain a measurement with the utmost precision, in much the same way as an adjustable spanner can be used today; and the component lug of the instrument was held in its place with a pin. Greater lengths were measured in units of the *chang* (=10 feet);* and there was a series of metrical units, progressing on a decimal system, for measuring volume (see p. 102). But for weights, the craftsmen and artisans had to work on the following, less regular series:

24 *shu* = 1 *liang*
16 *liang* = 1 *chin*
30 *chin* = 1 *chün*
4 *chün* = 1 *shih* (equivalent to 29·5 kilograms, 64½ lb.)

Some comparatively complex tools and devices had been evolved by the Han period. Jade had long been treasured as a highly valuable material, and had been shaped exquisitely for use at court ceremonies. Possibly even before the Han empire a circular knife had been used to cut through this hardest of stones; and there is one reference to the installation of this equipment in the workshops that were attached to the imperial palace. We do not know for certain how these early cutters were revolved, but the principle of continuous action by an operative device was perhaps being applied for other purposes. Towards the end of the Han period, if we may believe a somewhat questionable source, one ingenious inventor had set up a series of seven wheels, each measuring ten feet in diameter, which were worked so as to cool some of the palace quarters.

* There was also the 'pace' of six feet, which was used in linear measurements of land. See p. 166.

94 A wheelwright prepares and assembles the felloes, assisted by a woman (his wife?) with a baby on her back. A second craftsman is working with three containers, probably preparing glue or lacquer for the finished articles. An overseer, with a sword, supervises the work. From a relief found in east China

We are told that the wheels were interconnected and that the fans were operated by the labour of one man.

Very considerable skill was involved in making and assembling the component parts of Han wheels, and an extensive vocabulary testifies to the discrimination that a wheelwright needed to practise. He had to pay attention to using the right types of wood for the spokes or rims; the measurement of each component part had to be proportionate (e.g., the depth and thickness of the rim, the radius of the wheel and the length of the axle); and the complete article had to be fashioned with strength and stability. Here the Han artisans followed the example of their predecessors in shaping their wheels to be convex or concave rather than flat; for they knew that a carriage that ran on 'dish-shaped' wheels would travel more smoothly and securely than one whose wheels were shaped in a straight plane. The whole wheel and its attachments was a skilful complex of wooden and bronze parts. Lubricants were applied at points of friction and retained in their requisite situation by means of tightly fitting leather caps. Gear wheels or ratcheting was used when wheels were connected together, or perhaps in simpler devices such as pulleys. Material evidence includes an earthenware mould that was used for casting small gear wheels of 16 teeth; and there are several examples of toothed wheels of some two-centimetre diameter, cut with no less than 40 teeth.

As has been noted above (p. 175) pulleys were built into well-houses as a means of raising water, and the same techniques

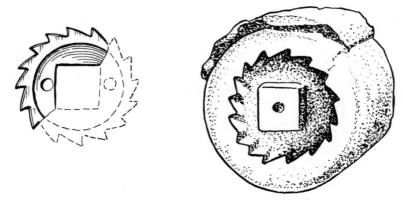

95 A cog-wheel and a mould used to manufacture another type

were probably used by signallers for raising flags or torches. The conveyance of water may often have been contrived by means of China's natural piping, in lengths of bamboo; but in the more sophisticated surroundings of the towns earthenware was used. There is some reason to believe that in the first century A.D., water-power was harnessed to activate the bellows on whose uninterrupted operation the iron-works depended; and we hear of certain water engineering works that were erected in about A.D. 190 to provide Lo-yang with a continuous and adequate supply of water. These latter devices may have been based on a series of high water-wheels. According to one statement the supply was sufficient to ensure that the streets of the city were sprayed or washed whenever this was necessary.

In addition there were other working projects which were marked more by an extravagant and unpractical use of manpower than by the systematic organisation of resources or the application of suitable equipment, although the references that we have to such undertakings are somewhat biased and cannot necessarily be accepted at their face value. Wang Fu, whose castigations have been encountered already, took exception to the use of highly expensive timbers for the construction of coffins. These were cut from trees that grew in the mountainous country south of the Yangtze River; they rose to enormous heights but took days to locate and months to hew. Crowds of coolies were needed to carry the trunks before they could be brought by oxen to the water's edge. Then the timber had to be conveyed long distances upstream before it reached Lo-yang, where the joiners and engravers could set to work; and this may have lasted for days and months. After all this wastage of labour the result was a single outer coffin, so heavy that it needed gangs of men to raise it and the largest of coaches for haulage.

This brief sketch of some of the industrial and technological achievements of the Han period must surely close with a tribute to the human contribution made by China's scientists and craftsmen, by her artists and inventors. Most of these pioneers are unknown to us by name, and we have glanced at some of their attainments already (see Chapter 8). We may perhaps conclude by noting that the heritage that they left has helped to mould the future development of Chinese society; to promote its growing enjoyment of material cultures; to increase its ability to withstand the forces of nature; and to deepen its understanding of nature's gifts.

Suggestions for further reading

For the general development of Chinese civilisation and the historical context of the Han period, readers are referred to *The Legacy of China* (edited by Raymond Dawson, Oxford, 1964); *A Short History of the Chinese People* (L. Carrington Goodrich, London, 1962); *Imperial China* (Michael Loewe, London, 1966); *East Asia: The Great Tradition* (Edwin O. Reischauer and John K. Fairbank, London, 1960); and *East Asia: The Modern Transformation* (John K. Fairbank, Edwin O. Reischauer and Albert M. Craig, London, 1965). For lengthier studies see *Science and Civilisation in China* (Joseph Needham and others, Cambridge 1954–   ), and a forthcoming corporate study which will be entitled *The Cambridge History of China* (Cambridge).

There are no textbooks in European languages which refer specifically and solely to the Han period. Translations of original source material are available in *History of the Former Han Dynasty* (Homer H. Dubs, Baltimore and London, 1938–55), where there are introductory statements to each reign and to select topics, and in *Records of the Grand Historian of China* (Burton Watson, New York, 1961). The introduction in *Food and Money in Ancient China* (Nancy Lee Swann, Princeton, 1950) refers to a number of aspects of political and economic organisation and practice. For military matters, see Michael Loewe, *Military Operations in the Han Period* (London, 1961) and *Records of Han Administration*, volume I (Cambridge, 1967), which is also concerned with the formulation and despatch of official documents. The subject of early methods of writing is discussed in *Written on Bamboo and Silk* (Tsuen-hsuin Tsien, Chicago, 1962). For the development of poetry, see *Sseu-ma Siang-jou* (Yves Hervouet, Paris, 1964); for intellectual trends, *A Short*

History of Chinese Philosophy (Fung Yu-lan, edited by Derk Bodde, New York, 1960); for religion, *Les Religions Chinoises* (Henri Maspero, Paris, 1950). Some recent archaeological discoveries are described in *Han Tomb Art of West China* (Richard C. Rudolph and Wen Yu, Berkeley, 1951); and for the arts, see William Willetts, *Chinese Art* (London, 1958) and *Foundations of Chinese Art from Neolithic Pottery to Modern Architecture* (London, 1965).

Material evidences of Han China can be seen in the British Museum, the Ashmolean Museum, Oxford, and the Fitzwilliam Museum, Cambridge, to name but three institutions in England.

Index

203